MORE MUSINGS

WITH DOT

By

Dorothy H. Killackey

Dedicated:

**To my Grandchildren,
Sean, Brian, Bobby, and Nicole**

Praise for Musings…...

"I thoroughly enjoy reading your stories and appreciate the values you share along with your personal experiences. Your story on virtues is a wake-up call for every generation to read." **Diana T.**

"I live in Loveland, Colorado, and a friend of mine in New York sent me your article about penny candy. It brought back so many memories, things from the recesses of my mind." **Maryann M.**

"Just got off the phone with Betty who said your book is the favorite of the readers and seniors in the nursing home. Even the nurses love the stories." **Janet K.**

"I look for your stories first when I get the paper. I'm a forty-five year old mom who appreciates your 'senior citizen' perspective on life." **Kiara L.**

"When I got your book for my birthday I found a shady spot and enjoyed reading it. I laughed and cried. Keep writing!" **Mary C.**

"Just wanted you to know your column is my favorite part of the local paper. This recent church supper installment totally transported me! I am thirty-seven years old and have always valued the past. You are really blessed that you got to experience that kind of community in your life. The food alone! Sounds amazing. Keep your articles coming!" **Stephanie S.**

Table of Contents

Part I: Memories of the Past

Part II: Personalities:

1. Cantankerous Carl (A Leader of Sorts)

2. He Came Back (The Past Interfering with the Present)

3. She Was Like a Rock (She's with the Angels)

4. I Didn't Do the Rhumba (Dating Dapper Danny)

5. My Best Friend Pat (Lost Confidentiality)

6. Grandpa (A Very Special Man)

Part III: Cultural Comments:

1.What's the Rush? (Let Them Have a Childhood)

2. Where Have the Old Virtues Gone? (The Media Is the Message)

3. Being "Gaslighted" (Light Influencing Emotions)

4. Musical Opiates (Dulling the Senses)

5. It's Confirmed, Big Brother Is Watching ("Brave New World")

6. Correction for Big Brother Column (In Our Libraries)

7. "Selfies", Word of the Year (Today's Narcissism)

8. Guns, Movies, Video Games (Letter to the Editor)

9. For Love of Country (Lost Patriotism)

10. Today's Music Giants (Grammy Awards)

11. Poisoning Our Children (With Pop Culture)

12. Where Is Love? (Relationships with Benefits)

13. Hope on the Horizon (Old-Fashioned Values)

Part IV: Personal Comments:

Seems Like Old Times

(A Sentimental Journey)

At eight years old, I began piano lessons. Every child in our family was expected to play piano. My great-grandparents in Germany had built pianos and my Aunt Dolly had a small miniature mahogany piano that Grandpa had built when she was a child. My Grandfather's occupation was repairing and tuning pianos. There was a "player-piano" in the living room that used music rolls, and I pumped the peddles for it to play wonderful popular and classic music. I loved doing that.

I've told of our vacations, staying one week at each grandmother's. When at Grandma and Grandpa B's, each evening was a "musical evening". My mother would "hit the keyboard" with her fast, twinkly notes, sometimes jazzing up music. Each uncle would play some instrument, and everyone sang. We kids accompanied with toy instruments from a big box. Grandma B. would skip around the floor with little dance steps, in between bringing out cold drinks and cookies.

I had learned that when my parents were about sixteen, the popular activity for young people was to gather around the piano and sing and dance to the latest "tin pan alley" songs. My mother, I was told, was shy, but, boy! could she improvise on the piano! If someone said the song was too high, she'd just start over at a lower key. Years later, when I asked my father why he chose my mother, he told me because she wasn't a "flapper" who wore dark red lipstick and short skirts. He loved her long dark hair worn in a bun, not a "boyish bob" like the other girls, and she was a "dynamite" piano player.

Well, back to my piano playing. I didn't like to practice, not one bit. I rose early every morning, before going to school, and practiced an hour before breakfast. My father would listen to my practicing and insist I go over every mistake ten times. This made the piano a terrible chore to me. Ten times, over and over the phrases that I played wrong! I hated the whole thing, but then, discipline was enforced strictly in our home, and, I soon learned to practice very slowly until I mastered the etudes, so that by the time I could pick up the tempo, I wasn't making mistakes. I got better, and in a few years was able to play simple editions of the classics and, at the year-end piano recital, I became the featured piano player. I didn't like the classics much. Probably because they didn't bring back the fun that we had, in those musical evenings at Grandma's.

By the time I was fourteen, my parents had accumulated a large box of toy instruments. I'd invite friends over to play the instruments and I'd accompany them on the piano. My father, always wanting to be in the middle of everything, made records of our "music" and one of the nerdy kids in the class, who was a kind of comedian, would be our announcer and make "jokes" introducing the "music". I enjoyed the piano in those days.

But, once college came, I stopped playing. In the dorm, serious musicians, training for Julliard, would practice at the grand piano.

I didn't dare bang out the popular music. And then, after college, and not living home, I didn't have a piano for another thirty years, and I lost "my touch". When I became a teacher, I'd play at a Christmas or special show that my class would be doing, but only in the last ten years, playing with the RSVP Chorus and Line Dancers at the Koehler Center in Mahopac, have I learned to enjoy playing my old songs again. Like old friends, playing is giving me so much pleasure! And those old songs, I'm in love with them all over again.

Fast Food in the Forties

(Using Self-Discipline for Success)

It was a cultural change for me, in the 1940's, coming from a quiet Pittsburgh suburb to the fast tempo of a New York City college. Freshman classes started at 8:00 am, dorm hours for freshmen were strictly enforced, and the city was fast-paced. People walked quickly, cars started and stopped quickly. Everything had an urgency to it. It was war time in the '40's, but New York City had always moved that way. It's no wonder "fast food" worked well for the bustling public.

The Horn and Hardart's "automat restaurants" had been in the city since 1914, and, New Yorkers loved them. Although, on entering, customers experienced a wild welcome of impressionistic color, these restaurants were organized and structured. I'd choose from delicious dishes like macaroni and pies, each dish contained in its own compartment. I'd put nickels into slots to open the sparkling clean glass doors with their chrome-plated knobs. Dishes were quickly replaced by "hands" from the kitchen. Food was always fresh as advertised, never kept overnight. Purchases could be bought to take home. The restaurant provided quick meals desired by an "on the go" public.

And then, near college, there was "Chock Full 'O Nuts" at the corner of Broadway and 116th Street, convenient for a quick cream cheese and nut sandwich with their extraordinary coffee and whole wheat donuts. (They advertised, "better coffee millionaire's money can't buy.") If I had to miss the dorm's meal, I could eat there before boarding the subway to go to the assigned museum or gallery trip required for a class project. Our professors taught us how to locate particular famous art objects, and then we were assigned a particular exhibit to find somewhere in the city and write about its location and description. By the end of week one, even a naïve student like me was unafraid of the city's transit systems. The college used the city as its cultural lab, and in the four years of college I learned to use its resources for assignments and for wonderful sight-seeing and pleasure.

But I can't talk about New York City food emporiums without mentioning Schraffts. Though not a fast-food place, it was the special restaurant to go to with your "maiden aunt" or grandmother. Schraffts had Irish waitresses in black and white uniforms, and they always served large desserts. In the "40's", a " lady" wore a hat and gloves when going to this restaurant, but, of course, any well-dressed lady always dressed up, shopping, going to interviews, or to work. We were told not to leave the school grounds in shorts or pants.

World War II changed everything. By the end of the war we seldom wore hats. They were replaced with flowers or headbands, (although job-seekers still conformed with hats.) The "new-look" came in (at least in New York City, though not in my hometown, Pittsburgh, for another two years. I knew I would be two years ahead in fashion when I went home for visits.) The "new-look" was to wear full, gathered skirts about two inches below the knee.

The fast living, fast food restaurants, fast pace of the city—it all was exhilarating, educational and "tuned in" to the times. This environment made me grow up, become independent.

It is a paradox. It would seem that such rules and "structure" would be inhibiting, but having discipline creates the "seeds" for creating a template, an individuality. When everything is allowed, nothing substantial is formulated. We need to give young people guidelines and self-control in living, like my parents and the college gave. Today adults have neglected directing young people. Young people want to "party". Our youth feel the need to cluster and confer with friends to make decisions. They can't make independent choices, never having been emancipated. In today's world, when everything is almost instantaneous, it's important to have a background of good guidance and self-direction.

At almost eighteen I had to learn to adapt to the new rules, to have the self-discipline needed for success. Maybe my strict parents were right after all, in their guidance. The fast-food restaurants were harbinger's of things to come, structured, reliable, with short waiting times. In today's world of instant news, swift decision-making and choices, discipline is needed. Maybe we should be educating our youth with this in mind. Other cultures have done this. Why don't we?

Church Suppers, Frieda's Fudgy Brownies, and Mom

(A Yearly Success)

I have wonderful memories of long ago church suppers and the excitement that went into those events. Always held in the middle of winter, the planning started right after the New Year. The event took weeks of preparation. Of course planning the food came first, even though the menu never changed, but, by first having the church ladies assemble in the parsonage, it was a special event in itself. The minister's wife, a tall, very homely "angel", was always dressed in her afternoon "best" for this occasion. A few of us teenagers passed out the homemade "treats", brought in for the occasion. The "Ladies Federation" members along with potential members were assembled to plan the upcoming "Supper". As a helper, I loved watching and listening to the ladies.

But, even with all the planning, Frieda's fudgy brownies, topped with whipped cream, would certainly be the dessert. This was accepted as the treat everyone waited for every year. Frieda, the church secretary, was a buxom single lady whose life had been dedicated to the church since it was first built. She had weathered three ministers and had been the confidant of their always weary, overworked wives. She was the ever-ready baby-sitter and haven in emergencies.

In early March, this "once a year event" gave the entire congregation, young and old alike, a chance to raise money to help pay the church's mortgage. My father, a very proud member of the parish, always sat at the door importantly with his "strong-box", taking the dollar bills and counting out change.

The older boys checked coats and men's hats as the men arrived, and, dressed in our best, we high school girls seated and served all comers. Other church members helped with the children, seating and placating them with small coloring books and crayons, to keep them busy while waiting for the special food treats.

As the hungry, expectant diners arrived and were seated, the red-faced, hair unkempt, church women took the steaming, oniony, cheese casseroles of scalloped potatoes out of the large ovens, and their men sliced succulent slabs of ham. Homemade applesauce and salads plus thick slices of homemade bread were also offered. And, last, but not least, Frieda's fudgy brownies, topped with ever-present whipped cream, were served with dark, rich, fragrant coffee.

But, besides those brownies, the highlight of the evening, after everyone was relaxed and totally sated, was my mother. She would slowly rise and shyly go to the piano to accompany old time favorite songs. Quiet as she was, everyone knew she could play the piano like no one else, changing key as needed, her fingers flying in rhythms and frantic, frenzied beats. Old Jim, a local tailor, helped along with his accordion, and Vincent, with his distinctive Irish tenor jollied us all along to "sing loud and clear". And, after playing all the songs printed on the song sheets, voices would ring out calling for other tunes, and certain uninhibited old-timers would be brought up to the microphone to share their favorite music, my mother always ready and able to nimbly accompany them! What a wonderful performance, particularly because this woman was a real treasure in their midst!

My mother's yearly piano mastery gave her the acceptance she had never had as a child. Her piano playing gave her ego the boost she had always needed. She never was the conversationalist that my father was, and she never was the fashion setter of the parish, but her music, her joy in sharing the beautiful past melodies at those church suppers in those cold, dreary winter months, gave my mother the boost and spirit to weather The Great Depression with all of its problems and worries. When I play the piano today, I know my Mom is "Up There", cheering me on! In my heart I know that my playing could never equal hers. And those wonderful old songs will always be there to warm and treat others to their old memories.

A Blizzard in My Past
(The 1936 Pittsburgh Flood)

Maybe it's the constant snow and bad driving conditions, or maybe it's being "cooped up" in the house so often this winter, but it reminds me of the great flood in Pittsburgh that was the result of the St. Patrick's Day Johnstown Flood of 1936. I had forgotten about that time, but this snow brings it all back.

Things were glum, during those years of The Great Depression. Remembering it now, our little family was luckier than so many. At least my father had a job, and, with being very careful about spending, we managed, my parents, my sister Betty, and me. I remember my father saying, "We have to tighten our belts and not eat quite so much." My mother put hot dogs in the split pea soup instead of the usual chunks of ham and, after school, a slice of "sugar bread" was our little treat instead of a cookie.

But on St. Patrick's Day, in 1936, sixty miles east of Pittsburgh, in a valley near the Alleghany, by the Little Conemaugh and Stony Creek Rivers, the dam above Johnstown was weakened by impounding water from icy floating logs and the dam did burst, flooding and "ruining Johnstown", as the historical annals tell. We lived in Mt. Lebanon, a Pittsburgh suburb, high up near Mt. Washington, over-looking "The Point", as they called where the Allegheny, Monongahela and Ohio Rivers came together. The Allegheny River rushed down to The Point, flooding the entire area, continuing through the city of Pittsburgh. And, much higher than The Point, the river continued to rise, flooding all the beautiful "department stores" and specialty shops in the city, water reaching as high as the fourth floor of Horne's Glamorous Department Store, as I remember.

In the suburbs, there were no utilities, no electricity, and no water. For several days we merely "existed" in the cold dark house, scooping up snow from outside and filling the bathtub to have water for making the toilet flush, and water for my father to shave. He still had to travel to his jobs. Blizzard conditions were outside, similar to what we have been having here this winter.

After a few days, my parents decided we must go somewhere to "wait out the storm" so that my father could wash properly and shave to go to his engineering jobs, rather than lose money staying home. My recollection was that he was called a "combustion engineer", and he had to travel extensively, checking blast furnaces for the local steel companies.

Betty and I were told to pack a few games and books to keep us occupied. Off we drove to a hotel high on Mt. Washington. I don't remember much about those hotel days except how closely my parents listened to the radio to hear the latest of the flooding conditions and for news that we could return home to electricity and our own beds.

Finally, the waters receded. No longer were people in canoes paddling up and down the main streets of Pittsburgh. Newspaper pictures slowed "filthy water lines" along the sides of formerly magnificent buildings. Trash and debris was disgusting and spewed over the town's streets. Streetcars couldn't function until roads were cleared of every kind of detritus.

With joy we finally packed up and drove home. Though our little house was bitterly cold, we were happy to be back, but we were in for a shocking surprise. Our bathtub was full of disgusting, greyish water, interspersed with chunks of brown soot. The formerly pure white snow that we had scooped up and put into the tub had melted! I will never forget my revulsion in seeing what the snow really contained. Pittsburgh, known then as the "smoky city", gave off volumes of soot and smoke with its blast furnaces and the purifying snowflakes cleaned the air. I would never eat snow again. I will never forget this period of my life.

Play It With Feeling

(Losing a Wonderful Teacher and Friend)

She was in my life for only about six months, but her influence alerted me to the vagaries in people. Mrs. Young was the church organist and my piano teacher. Our lessons were in the church basement. She was slender and only about 5'2", but her music held intense energy and emotion. I had had a very average piano teacher prior to Mrs. Young, a teacher who taught me the notes and necessary musical symbols, but when she moved, my parents hired Mrs. Young, whose patience and sweetness made me want to play well for her.

I began to practice extra hours, wanting to see her smile, but one day she stopped my playing an etude, and she told me to play it "with feeling". She demonstrated how to show "expression" in a piece. She explained that music was a kind of language, and just as we express ourselves in conversations, music is conveying "feelings" to the listener.

From that day on, I listened closely to her Sunday church "overtures" at the organ. I realized how she showed warmth and emotion as she played. The music took on meaning, and the more she played, the more I felt her solitude, her longings, maybe even her sadness. But I knew nothing about her as a person, as a woman.

Yes, only at about ten years old I was looking at people as individuals, wanting to know more about them. I was a close listener of the radio show "Grand Central Station", ("Crossroads to a million private lives!" the announcer told us.) I had begun to realize that everyone had their own story, and this intrigued me. I began to wonder about my teacher, Mrs. Young, and especially after closely listening to her music. I felt her passion and pathos as she played. Even at my young age I realized something that later became almost a "calling" to me, wanting to know why people were good or bad or kind or cruel.

Mrs. Young taught me for about six months. I began to love playing, and my technique seemed to please her. I hated to leave those weekly lessons.

But one day, when my father took me to my lesson, the door to the church basement was locked. There was not going to be a lesson. After we drove home, he called Mrs. Young's house, but no one answered! That Sunday a substitute played the organ at church. No one knew where Mrs. Young was. She was gone!

I was distressed when I heard of her leaving. Those weekly lessons had become important to me. She was my friend as well as my teacher. But one night, after going to bed, I heard my parents quietly talking downstairs about Mrs. Young. Someone at the church had seen Mrs. Young practicing her organ music and she was drinking liquor. They even saw the bottle. It was immediately brought to the attention of the Church Council President who declared this was unacceptable and she must be fired. And she was!

That sweet, understanding lady was fired for drinking! The shock I felt changed me. It disturbed my thinking as well as the meaning of so many things I had been taught about patience, understanding, loneliness. I never did find out about her life. Was she alone? Was she depressed? What made her drink?

This experience influenced my life's ambitions. No longer was I an innocent child. I began to look for reasons for sadness and heartache as well as joy and love of life. Searching for meaning in people's life-stories motivated me toward my psychology major in college and, after retiring from teaching, writing fifty biographies of seniors.

I've often wondered whatever happened to Mrs. Young. Where did she go and was she all alone? Couldn't someone have talked to her and understood whatever was troubling her? I do know that she profoundly influenced my life.

Creativity and Joy

(Inner Peace and Happiness)

At nine years old, aside from my best friend Helen, my closest pals became my paper dolls.

Helen and I cut out our first paper dolls, all named Jane Arden, from local newspapers, and we mounted our dolls on cardboard. The "Jane Dolls" came with a dress and coat and we colored our dolls and their outfits with my Mongol colored pencils.

Meanwhile, all over the country, paper dolls became commercially popular. Shirley Temple paper dolls (as well as real "Shirley" dolls) were favorites, and also the Dionne Quintuplets and Jane Withers dolls were sold. We preferred our newspaper dolls, not the commercial ones.

In time, a "teen-age paper doll" was printed that we cut out of the newspapers. We drew fancy outfits for her, like the smart suits and gowns that Ginger Rogers wore in the movies. Later, when "Gone with the Wind" was at the movie theater, Helen and I enjoyed seeing the old fashioned crinoline full skirts, the peplums, the shawls, the 1800's daytime wear and the ball gowns, and we copied the styles for our dolls.

We took old magazines and tucked our paper dolls between the pages, using separate sections for daytime, evening, and special events' outfits. Sometimes, Helen and I would trade these outfits. For example, two daytime outfits might be traded for one elegant ball gown. We then spent hours with those dolls, playing with them, pretending they were real dolls.

Meanwhile, boys saved soda caps and stuck those caps on their hats. Others collected colorful matchbook covers in cigar boxes. Back then, every store and establishment gave away matchbooks with bright advertising and eye-catching pictures and designs, popular, because people needed matches for their cigarettes or cigars. Almost every adult smoked. (And many of the boys smoked behind the school when no one was around.)

The 1930's were "depression days", and children didn't have a lot of toys. Plastic hadn't been invented yet. Many of the toy cars, trucks, doll house pieces were metal or wood and had, in the past, come from Japan or Germany, but Japan was then at war with China, and Germany wasn't worried about producing toys.

I smile as I remember the many hours spent designing, trading, and playing with those paper dolls. We were learning skills, matching colors and observing movie stars' fashions. We tried to carefully design our dolls' wardrobes so they'd be worthy of trading. Our designs became more and more flamboyant and creative as time passed.

I have been seeing a resurgence of paper dolls in "hobby stores", and I hope todays' young girls find the same pleasure that I remember. I hope they don't just cut out the outfits provided, but draw more clothes as we did. It doesn't take expensive equipment or a room full of toys to stir creative juices. If encouraged, most children will find a way to express their ideas.

Imagine my joy, when recently, my seven year old granddaughter, on her own, took an old sock and cut it up to make her doll a hat and coat! (The stocking's toe was the hat.) To think that she is like me, enjoying fashions and styles, and finding fun in creating a wardrobe for her dolls!

There are many ways children and adults can use their imagination, involving themselves in hobbies. There is a tremendous satisfaction in creating beauty for even the youngest child. It gives a sense of empowerment. Once felt, more creative juices stir, and they long to discover more. Restyling an old outfit, jotting down new thoughts, trying melodies out on an instrument, sketching a lovely scene or a beautiful image, conjuring up new, exciting ideas, all give an inner satisfaction. Once felt, there is no stopping. Turning to a hobby or creating something of beauty can be a haven in one's darkest days. I believe that sometimes, less outside stimulation is best, and the inside joy experienced can give happiness and inner peace.

Reminiscing About the Past
(Remember When?)

Every once in a while I see an article, an ad, that reminds me of the past. Don't get me wrong. I usually love living in the present, except when I get dismayed over politics and some of the contradictions that seem to be happening in the world today. But, it's often fun to remember the old days, remembering the things we took for granted. Sitting at a luncheon with other seniors, often those I don't really know, I love reminiscing with them. So often, they come from other cultures or other states or areas, and we have laughable variations on what we had and what we did in the past. I keep a collection of possible story ideas, and thumbing through the articles and odd slips of ideas I have jotted down, has given me material for "remembering when".

Do you happen to remember pan-cake make-up and veils on hats? I hated that make-up because, by evening, it tended to have deep cracks around the mouth from talking. But, maybe, by the end of the evening it didn't matter anyway. I had all shapes of hat-boxes on the shelf of my bedroom closet for the assortment of hats I wore to church. By the time World War II was over, hats were not as much in style, and we started wearing artificial flowers in our hair when we went out. Those girls in the "Mad Men" TV show are not too authentic with their hats, at least in New York City where I was. Maybe they kept wearing them in other parts of the country that always tended to be about two years behind New York City. (I'd go back visiting my parents in Pittsburgh, and be dressed in the latest, and the girls there hadn't heard yet of the new styles).

Does anyone remember dance-cards? At my first college dance in New York City, when there were four guys to every gal during the war, we were handed dance-cards and the boys signed up for dances. I doubt if anyone remembers them.

Remember "jitterbug jackets" that the guys wore with "pork-pie hats" when they were all "dolled up" for a date. Those jackets had wide shoulders and the shoulders often were a different color from the rest of the jacket. The "cool cats", as they liked to be called, often wore a long dangling key chain that went into their pocket. They had cloth handkerchiefs too that were carefully folded three or four times and showed out of the breast pocket.

Some girls wore their hair in "snoods", maybe fashioned from the women that worked, during World War II in the defense factories. There were colored lace snoods that enhanced their hair and matched their outfits. Spectator pumps for girls and two-toned shoes for the guys were worn with daytime outfits, and often a fluffy "jabot" peaked out from a tailored suit and fluffed around the neck.

Every girl wore either a garter-belt or girdle to hold up her stockings. The lovely silk stockings, that were worn before the war, disappeared. I was told the silk was to be used for the war's parachute-jumpers. The rayon stockings were awful. If the two garters on a stocking came open inadvertently, the stocking fell straight down, not clinging to the leg. Also, we constantly checked our stockings' seams to make sure they came straight up the back of the leg. There was a lot of preparation for an event or a date, when trying to look right.

But now, I read, old tie pins are adding sophistication to menswear. A colored "pocket-square" handkerchief is often added for conversation and style, sometimes to match a tie. Stacked-heel pumps with colored toes are a mod-style now too. Even open-toed dress shoes are back!

Maybe you can think of some other pieces of the past, like drive-in movies, juke boxes, and old comfy screened-in porches. It's fun sometimes to be nostalgic and even to admit to a very long ago past. I know I'm old and what they call "dated", but I wouldn't trade those happy innocent memories to what is happening with the date and fashion-scene today!

Live and Learn

(Goffstown, New Hampshire)

All of my training didn't prepare me to teach in that tiny, rural New Hampshire school. World War II was over and my husband was attending local St. Anselm's College. The town's uniform factory was shut and there were few jobs locally, but, this New Hampshire school district needed a teacher, and I was happy to be hired at $2,000 for the school year or $200 a month. My fifth grade classroom had ten-year-old children and ten-year-old text books, plus a syllabus for me, but not much else. At least there was a blackboard and bulletin board. I could see this was going to be a real challenge.

My students were mostly farm children, with few books in their homes, and not much concern about learning. But they were good kids, and I was an energetic twenty-three year old. At least the children brought their own loose leaf notebooks, so they had paper. I was expected to teach fifth grade subjects, but also I had to teach art, music, and gym classes, as well as be outside at recess.

Music was easy. An ancient piano, lacking two keys, was in the music room, and we all enjoyed singing the "old songs". I taught them to read music and sing harmony, anticipating a "parent show" in the future.

Recess was bitter cold, often below zero, but afterwards we'd trudge in for the cafeteria's hot chowder, and of course I ate with the class.

Teaching gym worried me. I never was very athletic, but I discovered some long-forgotten square dance records in the "resource room"! What a find! These would be for my gym classes. The children loved the record caller's "do-ce-do's" and the loud, rousing music, and I even joined in the dancing.

But art! We were offered books of wall paper samples that a local shop owner didn't want. We used these for projects, using imagination, and I decorated the room with their creations. And, on regular mimeograph paper, the children drew "self-portraits", labeling the pictures with an "Old English type print" that I taught them. These covered the bulletin board.

As spring drew near, I decided that our final project would be to design and create a little town, to be laid out on an old table from the supply room. We hoped it would be exhibited in the main school lobby. We took strips of newspapers and wadded them up with paste made from flour and water, and created a kind of "papier mache". They designed a town like their own Goffstown. They fashioned stores, churches, little houses, and even people. We all agreed that it was beautiful.

There was a week's spring vacation and then school resumed. When I opened the classroom door I was almost "knocked over" by the disgusting stench emanating from the room. There was a horrible greenish mold all over our "papier mache" town! Over the vacation, in the warm closed room, mold had grown and covered our village display. Our town was a total loss! We had to share another classroom for the week that it took to air out! The wonderful project was a disastrous mess. The class and I had learned that flour and water paste can get moldy.

I led the disappointed children in a discussion about this upsetting situation, and then assigned them to write stories about the experience. I stressed the fact that all of our hopes don't always turn out, and we can learn more from our mistakes than from our triumphs. It was an important "life lesson" for them.

At the end of that school year, I was pleasantly surprised when my principal asked me to return for the next school year, and I was happy to hear that the parents of this class had requested that I come back as their children's sixth grade teacher! My year was a success after all.

After the Fall

(or Sixty-Five Years After Barnard)

It was 9:15 am Monday morning and the heads of twenty-five fourth graders were bent over their desks working on the day's first assignment. I sat, perched high on a desk in the back of the room, looking over plans for the day, when I pitched forward into blackness. Then, dizzy and reeling, I tried to raise myself, and then blackness again.

When I came to, the school nurse was bending over me, and the wide-eyed, scared children were crowding around. I vaguely remember a stretcher and an ambulance.

On the fourth morning in the hospital, the night nurse came and said, "We know now what happened. You need a pacemaker. Overnight you "flat-lined" for four minutes." My right shoulder was fitted with a special battery that forced my heart to beat properly. My life was to be different from then on. Why didn't I stay dead when I "flat-lined"? I had to find out.

I had never been especially philosophical about life, but now I felt forced to find a reason for living. I applied for retirement to change my focus. It wasn't that teaching wasn't fulfilling. I loved it. It was that I had to figure what I must do.

After retirement I sold real estate for fifteen years. This work gave me flexible hours; I could work hard or be relaxed, meeting people, enjoying the new houses I showed, and having time for volunteering.

During those real estate years, I worked with the Office of Aging writing fifty senior's biographies, awarding certificates and corsages at ceremonies, celebrating lives of those dedicated seniors who used their declining years to help others. I made wonderful friends, old timers who had never been noticed. From the poorest to the wealthiest, all had been influenced by someone, not necessarily a parent, who became mentors. These seniors poured out their stories that weren't always pretty, but needed to be told.

In time, I joined volunteer groups, working with people who unselfishly did for others, for the joy of it, not for fame or power. I branched out in writing, doing articles about these groups of volunteers, enjoying the bit of publicity I could give them. I worked with the Children's Committee, the local library, an honorary teacher's group, and the SeniorNet computer techies.

One day the editor of the local weekly paper asked if I would write a column to voice my thoughts. She gave me free reign to write anything I felt was worthy of discussing. I asked her if she meant "my musings". "Yes," she said, "and we will call it that."

For over two years my stories have been published. I am stopped by strangers asking if I really mean what the latest column has said. I am told my columns are sought out by a vast number of senior citizens in our county, and they, in turn are mailing them everywhere.

Yes, my book, now published, called "Musings", is a compilation of fifty-four of those essays. An Amazon publisher had approached me and asked to publish it. Twenty five years after fainting in the classroom, I know what I must do. I must pass on the joy and fulfillment of helping others. I must tell others to live with their pain and aches and help each other. I must use my eighty-five years of experiences to encourage others to celebrate their old age and share their life stories. We need each other.

Remember Housedresses?

(Moms Wore Them)

I'll bet a lot of my readers don't even know what a "housedress" is. Back in the 30's and early 40's moms stayed home and did housework, made meals, baked, and washed laundry. (However, in the teaching profession, in the 30's and earlier, if a teacher got married she was asked to leave the job. It was Depression time, and jobs being scarce, there was to be only one "bread-winner" at a time in a family.) The moms and other women who were doing "housework" wore housedresses, usually of a cotton percale print and without much shape. They usually wore an apron too, to prevent spots. If you remember actress Edna Best in the old 30's movies, she made an acting career being someone's servant or mother and always wearing a housedress. Hattie MacDaniel was another actress always in her housedress.

Every year, for Christmas, my mother gave my grandmother's two housedresses each. I thought these were dismal presents and I asked her why not something nicer like candy or a pretty scarf. She told me that's what they could use and what they wanted.

This woke me up to what they meant by "woman's place was in the home". What a dreary thought to me, a teenager. And I said so. She explained that I should become a career girl if I didn't want that future and that all married women were expected to be homemakers.

In seventh grade all the girls took one term of cooking and one term of sewing. After cooking class we'd bring out "samples" of our work and share them with boys in the class that we liked. Those classes were called "homemaker classes" because we were being trained for just that, to be homemakers. Boys took one term of woodshop and one term of car repair because they were expected to someday be the "men of the family".

I have to admit, those homemaker classes were perfect for me. I hated the ugly homemade dresses my mother made for me, and I learned to make my own skirts that we all wore with sweaters. I learned too about baking, something my mother didn't do, and I've used those baking hints and skills all my life.

But, back to those housedresses. We were even taught to make them! I'll never forget the roses on the percale material and the Singer Sewing Machine pattern. The teacher was so very particular, but the sewing skills she taught me were valuable for when I was in college and I made my own gowns for proms. On summer vacations from college I'd tackle the project of a new prom gown. It was much cheaper than buying those gowns and I proudly became pretty skillful.

It's funny how skills we pick up as children can become useful as we venture into new avenues. A college assignment for my psychology major, five years after those sewing classes, I was assigned to work with poor children in a "settlement house" in lower New York City. I taught those children to sew and even mend their clothes. And even later, in my first real job, working with little girls recuperating from rheumatic fever, I taught them to make doll dresses.

But World War II changed it all. Men were called to the services and women were needed out there. Everyone's heard of Rosy the Riveter, but girls and women were hired for everything, and it was changed so that teachers could even stay on if married. A few years into the war any young man not wearing a uniform or who was old was sure to wear a lapel pin showing he was discharged from the service. Even respectable women started to leave the housework to someone less educated, and they started taking "brush-up courses" and getting college degrees. Housedresses were tossed out, except for the few who wanted (or had to) stay home.

I wonder if anyone out there still wears one.

My Favorite Things
(Enjoying the Special Things In Life)

I guess we all have important things and activities that help us through tough times and that we enjoy. Of course, nothing beats having coffee and cake with special friends. Just being able to talk freely and not be misunderstood is so relaxing. But I'm now musing over important items that aid and help me. I'll bet the reader has his own list.

My comb is a favorite, even though it has two teeth missing, but I like it because it is heavy with strong teeth. The missing teeth broke years ago when I dropped the comb, but it hasn't stopped me from using it. It was given to me many years ago by a retiring hairdresser friend. No other comb combs my hair as nicely. And what would I do without my hairdryer! I can set my hair, and, when I use it correctly, I don't need curlers or bobby pins to get the wave I want. Over twenty years ago a dear friend gave me this.

Years ago I saw actor Joel McCrea in a movie wearing a shawled sweater. I loved the warm, cozy look it gave Joel in his Far North movie. When I saw one later in the store, I bought it, a gray tweed, shawled style, and it really is cozy warm. It's one of the first things I put on when returning home in winter time, along with my comfortable shoes. I wrote about them in an old story and how I am joining other old people, whose feet hurt when wearing more popular styles. Of course I wouldn't want anyone but my dearest friends to see me, but dear friends don't care what I'm wearing.

My old purple bathrobe can't be forgotten. It's at least two sizes too big, but it has comforted me through colds and flu and shingles with its coziness, even though it's old, and some people would call it shabby. I got it from one of my children many many years ago. It was almost thrown out but I rescued it. There's nothing like relaxing in my favorite comfy chair when I'm wearing it!

When I go to visit my daughters I always bring my favorite knife for cutting and pealing vegetables and fruit. I like to help them make dinner and that knife feels perfect in my hand for helping in the kitchen. If I use their paring or cutting knives I never can do a good job. My favorite spatula is a treasure to me. It handles perfectly in scraping out every speck of the cookie or cake dough and it even handles high temperatures if using it with the frying pan. For years I suffered with floppy spatulas that couldn't handle high-heat. This one is perfect.

When they finally pack me up to go to a nursing home, I'll put on my comfortable shoes and grab my shawled sweater. I guess my bathrobe will finally be tossed away and they'll have me bring my never-worn red bathrobe that's been hanging in the closet since someone gave it to me as a present. I know they won't let me take my knife or spatula, but maybe I can bring my hairdryer, and I'll certainly take my comb. I can't imagine any future chair fitting me as nicely as my old chair, but then no place would be as nice to end up in as would home.

Special, favorite things are like good old friends. We love them dearly. They comfort us and make the day pleasant, sometimes even relieving those ever-present aches and reminders that we aren't getting younger. I'm going in now to cozy up in my bathrobe and sit in my favorite chair. Maybe there's a chocolate bar in my dresser drawer!

Letting Your Hair Down
(Terri's Beauty Parlor)

Growing up, I never went to beauty parlors and neither did my mother. I'll always remember her long dark brown hair that she coiled into a bun at the base of her neck. Her hair was wavy up to the bun, and neat, and she kept mine that way too. She'd put lemon juice into the rinse water after washing my hair, to "give my light brown hair a glisten", she said. I wore braids until around thirteen, when I finally just chopped them off, without permission, and considered myself emancipated. When I think back, I'm surprised that my strict parents didn't object to this.

Well, with shorter hair, I experimented with hairdos, using combs to hold my hair back at the sides, and finally, in college, settled with a fairly attractive hairdo, always, keeping my wavy hair long, about half-way down my back. When I had my babies, I just pulled it into a "pony-tail".

Not until my thirties was my hair cut, and it was my landlady, a retired beautician, who suggested that she style and shape my hair "to make me look my age". After that, during teaching days, I'd venture into a beauty parlor to have someone thin and trim my hair. But I never stayed around to experience the "world in itself" of a beauty parlor. That all changed when I met Terri.

One day, during my second career in real estate, it was my "uptime" at the agency. A very distressed-looking lovely lady came in, saying she needed a rental. Her beautiful eyes showed the desperation that I had recognized in so many children in the past, as I offered to help her. Her home had totally burnt down and she had only the clothes she was wearing. The toaster hadn't been unplugged the night before, which started a fire, and she woke up in a sea of smoke, only able to escape flames by climbing out through an upstairs window. Everything was lost.

It was pure luck that I had just gotten a "rental listing" the day before and I took her to see the condo apartment that became her shelter for the next six months until her house was rebuilt. I felt so badly for her that, to comfort her, I brought over an afghan that I had just finished crocheting, so that she had a little warmth. As we talked, I discovered she had her own business, "Images", and I asked if she could restyle my hair.

This all happened over fourteen years ago. Terri and I became friends from that day. From then on I became a part of the beauty parlor world, where Terri and her staff truly transform unruly hair for women of all ages, into a lovely frame for their faces. I know now what is meant by "letting your hair down" because that is what women and girls do in beauty parlors. Everything and anything is talked about, cried over, giggled over, discussed.

I'm sure in men's barber shops the same thing goes on, but it can't possibly be as intimate as this woman's world where anything goes. Operations are discussed, boyfriends are described, ailments and sleepless nights are pondered, successes are applauded, and women can be themselves as they can't be anywhere else! The old expression "letting your hair down" had to have started in such a special woman's world. It is a haven, a sanctuary, where women become friends and understand and help each other.

Yes, over fourteen years ago I discovered this, and I have been getting my hair cut and styled by Terri and Linda there ever since. Terri still tells customers about our meeting and she still treasures the afghan I gave her. But then, she gave me something even nicer, a haven and a good friend who councils me, and cares about the hundreds of faithful customers who wouldn't go anywhere else to "let down their hair".

My "Robbie Christmas Tree"

(A Second Grade to Remember)

My little three-foot Christmas tree is finally decorated and resting on a stand in my large front window. For twenty-seven years it has sparkled there with colorful lights, and has guided friends to my door. But that little tree is more than a Christmas decoration to me. It's my "Robbie Tree", a gift and an inspiration from forty-five years ago.

Back then I was a fledgling second grade teacher. Before that school year started I was nervous about a student, Robbie, who was scheduled to be in my class. Kindergarten and first grade records warned me of his obstinacy, uncooperative behavior and lack of any discipline.

From day one, this tall, very bright child was ready to challenge me. At recess time I took him aside and asked if he thought he could read well enough to help me by getting information for me in the library. "Read well enough!" he said. Well, he took my challenge and, after lunch, he trotted down to the library and looked up "sharks", as I asked, and returned to class loaded with information. I asked him to report his findings. He had fifteen minutes to literally teach us all about sharks. It was a win-win situation! The class was mesmerized! He had been their nemesis on the playground and in previous classes. After his report, I gave him the credit he deserved, and, from then on, we were off to a great start.

I tutored Robby to be my class aide. He put papers in order for me, filed our "class library collection", put up bulletin boards, all the while "acing" the class assignments and tests.

After the first week, Robbie's mother came in to see me, overjoyed at the change in him. In thanks, December 1st she brought me a three foot artificial tree, to put up for the class to decorate. From that day on, during the last half hour of each school day, the class dedicated themselves into making our little tree a real creation. I brought in aluminum foil that they squeezed into balls and strung across the boughs. Robbie gave us a report on birds, and so, with "bird patterns" that I made out of cardboard, they traced birds and colored them brightly and strung dozens of birds onto the tree. I showed them how to cut out snowflakes in delicate patterns and they went on the tree too. Each child drew an elf, and they made holiday "Elf Cards" for their parents. Their Elf promised on his card a "giving gift" to a family member. We listed possible gifts they could "give", like setting the table each night, drying the dishes, picking up their clothes, folding the laundry, letting Mommy get a long Saturday sleep, or taking out the garbage. (These are choices they thought of.) Robbie posted these Elf Cards on our snow-flake- rimmed Holiday Bulletin Board. I taught them to sing "Winter Wonderland" and "Silver Bells" and we laughed and enjoyed singing each evening, while waiting for the buses to go home.

For the next ten years my classes trimmed that "Robbie Tree", each class being creative and deciding their own "themes" for

45

patterns and the decorations, until the day came when schools weren't allowed to decorate for the holiday, and so I brought my little tree home and stored it in my attic.

That had been a memorable year for me with Robbie in my class. He had been challenged for the first time, and he had shown his wonderful learning potential. He began to love school, and I learned, first hand, that every child has his own mode and ability to learn and should be taught accordingly. Robbie's year with me was an education for both of us.

Every year I think of Robbie as I set up the little tree. And yes, as you would expect, Robbie went on to higher educational heights and is now a translator in Israel.

On With the Show!

(Dancing Dottie)

All those wonderful old movies like "Forty-Second Street" and "Broadway Melody of 1933" now shown on TV inspire me to write about my own experiences eighty years ago! In my earlier story, "So I Thought I Could Dance!", I told of being little "Dancing Dottie", one of a troupe of entertainers from the Johnson Dance Studio. Little Billy Paul was my partner, and we were trained to do dance routines like being "Bell-Hops" or being bride and groom in a "Tom Thumb Wedding". I have old "glossy pictures" from the display cases that were outside the theaters. In one of my tap dance routines with Billy in a tux, I wore a velvet, bare-backed, sequined gown, sophisticated, slinky, down to my ankles. In the "bell-hop number" we wore snazzy white uniforms trimmed with gold buttons and epaulettes and cocky square hats perched on our heads. It's a wonder that I still remember from eighty years ago, and we were only five years old!

I have no idea what made my parents enroll me in dancing school. I do know that Mrs. Johnson formed the troupe back in 1932, and arranged performances at Shriners' meetings and hospitals all over Western Pennsylvania. I think it was to raise money for their causes. I remember the excitement of the huge standing applause Billy and I got after our acts. Just our youth would engender the praise. Remember too, the movies showed child actors Shirley Temple and Jane Withers as well as "Our Gang".

I remember our final performance, called "Pittsburgh On Parade", at the great Stanley Theater in Pittsburgh when Dick Powell starred , heading the large cast that was pulled in from local dancing schools. The chorus girls backstage coddled and cooed over me, my being the youngest of the entertainers. They put "grease-paint" (an early entertainer's version of leg make-up) on my legs for the bell-hop routine, and bought me ice-pops from a local vendor. I loved watching the girls "touch up" their make-up between acts. I still remember the excitement as the entertainers raced onto the stage coming down the stairs from the overhead "cat-walks" and balconies from their dressing rooms.

After that gala show, most of Mrs. Johnson's troupe went on to Hollywood, along with Dick Powell, who became a musical movie star and later did dramatic movies. He was so kind to me. I will always remember his example of encouraging the cast with his up-beat attitude. Just developing and practicing the acts was exciting, and must have taught me about show business. (My earlier "musings" story explained my parent's opting out of letting me go with the troupe to Hollywood)

Why would I "muse" over those days? I now realize how that experience, young as I was, influenced me. From then on, I was always ready for doing a show. I entered every contest at school and actually won once, singing "Polly Wolly Doodle". I joined choral groups, acting groups, and organized a show every chance I got.

Even in my first New Hampshire teaching days, I had my fifth graders do a South American show they wrote and "produced" for their parents, "building" cardboard rubber trees, doing "La Cucaracha" dancing and singing Latin-type songs. Years later, teaching in Brewster, New York, I had my classes make their own puppets and give shows every year, until the auditorium finally became a classroom from lack of space, and the shows had to stop.

I write this to encourage parents and those who work with children to do plays and dramatics. Having those experiences taught me to be unafraid of performing and unafraid of conducting meetings. I learned early to project my voice and to take charge of community events. Letting children perform and encouraging their "show and tell" times will give them the strength and courage for speaking out and give them leadership skills for the rest of their lives.

"Is That All There Is?"

(Singer Peggy Lee)

Yes, you might have recognized the title, "Is That All There Is?" because it was a great song, sung by singer/artist /songwriter, Peggy Lee. When I looked her up on "Google" she was described as a "sophisticated persona". She sang with Benny Goodman and his band from 1941, and was famous for such songs as "Why Don't You Do Right?" and "Manana Is Good Enough for Me" and "Fever". She was considered by many as the most influential jazz vocalist of all time.

Peggy Lee was what young people today would call "Drop Dead Beautiful", tall, statuesque, voluptuous, poised, everything I wished I was. As I was growing up in a Pittsburgh suburb, just beginning to date Bill, who was two years older than me, one of the special dates I remember was taking the streetcar to Pittsburgh and the Stanley Theater, and attending a show with Benny Goodman, staring Peggy Lee. In those days I didn't know anything about jazz music and Eddie Condon's in Greenwich Village in New York City. I didn't know one trombone from another or who the instrumentalists were. Bunny Barrigan, Claude Thornhill, Gene Krupa, all were new names to me. And to attend a "big band concert" featuring Peggy Lee—well, I was going with Bill, who was 17 and knowledgeable about jazz because his father played clarinet in a band and Bill had all the latest records.

The concert was heaven to Bill, but to me was awful. I came back feeling ugly, knowing I was a "dud" compared to Peggy Lee. There, on the stage was gorgeous Peggy Lee, wearing a different beautiful gown with each new song, gowns that slithered and shimmered down her perfect, mature figure. Her white-blond hair piled high and her alabaster-smooth face with those deep blue eyes, singing in her special, thoughtful, effortless style. There was no screaming or jumping around in the audience as we have today. The audience was mesmerized with her words that seemed to be focused on each male listener, and only him. Her singing was personal, conveying her mood and innermost feelings. I wish concert goers today could, just once, experience the way she transferred her longings, joy, and pain in her music. The manic screamings of today's performers, holding tightly to their microphones, their jumping around, often suggestively gyrating and motioning, are not art. Their "music" is an assault on my ears and sensibilities.

As I think back on those teenage years and how insecure and vulnerable I was, not giving myself credit for what I was and could be, I have to stop and think about young people today. I didn't appreciate my youth and good health, my energy, all the things I was blessed with. I never thought about others who weren't as lucky, some even with physical problems. I was self-centered and jealous of that beautiful woman on the stage. Bill's eyes were only for the lovely Peggy, and I felt ignored.

But why do I write about my long-ago self-centered, immature stage? As I read about Peggy Lee, who I disliked because she "showed me up" when I was a foolish teenager, I learn how Peggy Lee lived a long life, to age 81, and suffered greatly from diabetes. Her beauty and talents didn't give her happiness. She had four marriages and a great deal of personal and physical suffering. When I reflect, I realize that Peggy Lee, only six years older than I, would probably give all of her talents, wealth and fame for the happy, healthy years I had, and the relatively good health and dear friends I knew.

Peggy Lee sang "Is That All There Is?", and I wonder if she was thinking how barren her life was, as she sang, even with all its glitter and fame. The irony is, as I was jealous at her power over my date, was I the one who was really blessed with a long productive happy future, not Peggy? I didn't realize how lucky I was. All I could see was the present. When did I start to "muse" about life?

A Penny For Your Candy

(Sweet Memories of the 30's & 40"s)

When I recently read of the death of Lillian Jacobs at the age of 102 years, the caption told of her family's candy shop at East 84th Street in New York City. Penny candy was their specialty. I was intrigued and had to read on. The shop sold specialties like paper strips with colored candy buttons and pastel-colored wax milk bottles containing a luscious liquid. Memories flooded my mind. Indeed, I knew I must write about this.

In the thirties and forties, on Saturday mornings, the local movie theaters showed "serials" before the main movie feature. The movie ticket was only a dime for children. All week my friends and I saved the pennies that we earned doing chores, to go to the movies and to Maxey's, the penny candy store next to the theater, for our bag of candy that we'd linger over during "Tail-Spin Tommy" or "Buck Rogers in the 20th Century". I loved the jaw-breakers that I'd suck and make last through the whole episode. Then there were the little red or black licorice hats and "red hot dollars". My sister Betty loved the chocolate babies, and Bobby, our neighbor, always bought the picture cards of American "Indians" like Tacumseh wrapped with a square of gum. We loved savoring our bag of candy. The main movie feature was never as important as the morning serial attraction.

So many old experiences will be lost if not recorded by us "old souls". In those old days, when there was no television, children would rush home from school, anxious to first finish chores or homework to turn on the radio to their favorite series. For me it was "Little Orphan Annie" with her dog Sandy, the faithful servant Punjab, and Daddy Warbucks. I always wanted one of those "Annie Shake-Up Mugs" and the secret decoder rings that Ovaltine coupons could bring. I wished I could decode the messages given at the end of each show, but I had to settle for just listening to each story. Mom said Ovaltine was too expensive, but, years later, in my sixties, I finally bought chocolate Ovaltine. I think wishing for it made it more delicious than it really was.

Another special radio show was "Let's Pretend". The fairy tales that were enacted and the wonderful classical musical backgrounds made Saturday mornings a time I looked forward to. But then, the song "When It's Roundup Time in Texas" will always make me think of Ralston Cereal, and I loved "Jack Armstrong, the All American Boy" sponsored by Wheaties! Evenings I would listen to "I Love a Mystery" with Jack, Doc, and Reggie and their adventures.

When I was sick and home from school, my Mom turned on the "soap operas" that she listened to while she cleaned, cooked, and baked. "Ma Perkins", "Stella Dallas", and "Back Stage Wife" are ones I remember. And, as a young lonely bride in New Hampshire in the early 1950's, with no TV, the radio personalities Bob and Ray gave me chuckles and lightened my world.

Somehow, children's programs today don't have the wonderment, the mystery, the fun, that I experienced all through grade school, listening to those programs. They gave me mental pictures and imaginings that totally took me out of the mundane, the homework, the chores, the have-to's of life. And I couldn't listen just any time, but had to have homework done, room picked up, the supper table set, to relax for my 5 o'clock shows.

In later years, on Saturday nights, while in my teens, I listened to "The Hit Parade" every week, I learned all the words to the latest songs. And when I started dating, that same music was the background music for getting dressed to go out.

Those old memories are sweet. They block out the tough life of the Depression Days for me. I know money was a worry for the adults, as well as crime and politics. I know why they call it "The Depression". The country was truly depressed in mind and spirit. And then came "The War"! All of life changed! But, Penny Candy and Radio Days cushioned my life and made those memories poignant.

The Fuller Brush Man

(Or, The Men Who Came Around)

Years ago there was a movie about "The Fuller Brush Man", and I think the actor Red Skelton was its star. But, even earlier, when I was a little girl in a suburb of Pittsburgh, PA, I remember the Fuller Brush Man coming to our door, probably twice a year, selling brushes and cleaning products to my mother. She never drove, most women didn't, and so she was happy to have someone come to the house with cleaning products. The man would come into our hallway and lay out a large cloth and display his products.

Recently, a friend of mine was remembering how in the Westchester area, in the 30's, there was a traveling man who sold all sorts of clothing, men's, women's, children's. If he didn't have your housedress size, he'd come back the next day with it. He sold men's pants, shirts, socks, underwear, and women's aprons and nightgowns. Of course, in those days, people also ordered necessary things from the Sears Roebuck Catalogue.

Even earlier than the 1930's, there were no frost-free refrigerators, and a lot of people had "ice-boxes" to keep their food cold. The iceman drove around supplying big chunks of ice to keep the icebox cold, and, they tell me, little boys ran after the truck to retrieve the chunks of ice that fell off his truck. And, I heard that in some areas there were "Junk Men" and "Fish Peddlers" who came around, even men selling seltzer. Some areas had a "Scissors Grinder", a man who carried a sharpener on his back and would sharpen knives and scissors where needed. I guess any enterprising man was able to make a living selling what an area needed.

There were other "traveling salespeople", but my mother was afraid of opening the door until she first peeked out the side window and recognized someone. She told me about the time, when she was little, living in The Bronx, NY, people worried about gypsies who had a bad reputation for stealing. But then, we never saw gypsies in my Pittsburgh neighborhood.

I remember, as a teenager, selling Christmas cards to benefit our church. My sister and I walked miles around our little suburb, taking orders and later delivering them. In those days there was never the worry about children being kidnapped where we lived. We even played outside on the street, in the summers, until the street lights came on, and then we had to go home. We had wonderful times playing Hop Scotch, Kick the Can, Jump Rope, Who's It? No one had to walk their children to school then, or to the school bus.

How different it is today! TV tells us of small children walking to the bus, being picked up by strangers. We are all alerted to predators and dangers. Where did they come from? Did I just live in a very safe area? Did children just have more freedom? I was warned never to talk to strangers, but no strangers ever approached me.

Is it that cities and towns are more crowded so more deviant people are walking around? Is it that I was just lucky to be living in a nice area? Are people today more disturbed and more prone to anti-social activities? Why isn't it safe anymore? Is there too much pressure and people breaking down under it?

I know that schools can't discipline as they did in the past. My father always told me, "The teacher knows best?" I know that we are more a "mixed society" than before and so people aren't "watching out" for others and protecting others as much. I see that you can't tell by people's clothing whether they are good or bad because even the rich wear weathered jeans and sloppy looking outfits. Maybe we are too crowded and the police can't arrest all the suspicious looking people. "Who Changed the Rules?" That was a story in my "Musings, Book I". I often think about this.

Where's Betty?

(Drugs in the '40's)

I was a college freshman in the "40's" in New York City. The rules at the school were strict and the tests were daunting. A high grade average had to be maintained in order to stay, and low grades put a student on probation with the possibility of not continuing with the class.

It was during the mid-year exam period. Six of us girls had become friends since the first day of school. We were from all over the country and we were awed with being in the World War II hustle/bustle of New York City. We laughed, joked, and gossiped, meeting for lunch each day in the dorm's cafeteria. And, when the mid-year exams were scheduled, we worried over the tests together, planning to meet there afterwards to relax. The tests had been scheduled in different classrooms of the college, to accommodate over three hundred freshmen. We planned a noontime meeting.

Five of us met at noon, but where was Betty? We lingered with lunch, getting more worried as time passed. Despite our other afternoon plans, we went up to the dorm's third floor, looking for her at her room.

Betty's room was locked, but we noticed light in the old-fashioned upper transom window. Something was wrong! The dorm-mother was called and she used her key to open the door. Only barely breathing and in a coma, Betty was sprawled across the bed! On the night table was a "No-Doz" empty pill bottle! She had taken the pills to stay awake for cramming! We had no idea where she could have gotten those pills! (We remembered the rumors of truck drivers using No-Doz to stay awake on long trips.) We stayed with her until the ambulance arrived. In our grief we saw them take her away. We tried to comfort each other and understand what had happened.

I never saw Betty again. She wasn't allowed visitors, and her family eventually took her home to Boston where she went through intensive counseling. She returned to college there.

I still feel the horror that filled me when I saw Betty's limp body. It's now decades later, but this left an indelible impression on me. "Why", I asked myself, did she have to resort to those powerful pills?

In those days we wondered where Betty was. We looked for her and found her almost dead body. But, in my musings today, I ask myself where was she mentally that would make her go to such an extreme? I ask that also about our young who take drugs or drink too much. What internally drives them to satisfy problems, thinking they must depend on drugs or drink instead of rational reasoning? Are they so insecure and unsure of themselves, as Betty probably was? Perhaps being a doctor's daughter she felt pressure to succeed. We blame the drug pushers, but thousands of buyers are out there for them.

Where are the families in giving advice or problem solving? Do young people have someone to talk to, someone understanding, who can help satisfy worries and wonderings? Is their family too "busy" or too wrapped up in their own lives to see changes in behavior, and help with problems as they arise?

I worry too about the loved ones of those who are hooked on drugs or drink. Their once comfortable lives change. The "users' " lives will never again be the same, but their families' lives are also drastically affected.

We want the drug "pushers" off the streets and out of our neighborhoods, but when will we be ready to stop to help those insecure young people, those who need our understanding, not drugs, to conquer their fears? They might act cocky and think they are "with it" socially, to be in the drug scene, but maturity and just having someone there might give them the backbone to say no to their peers and to temptation.

Cantankerous Carl

(A Leader of Sorts)

Composing biographies was my first step into serious writing. Years ago, when a friend needed a gluten-free diet, we needed a dietician's advice. I had heard that the Putnam County Offices for Aging were excellent for seniors needing help. I called ahead, and was greeted by the dietician, and after getting her help, I met the office's director who had been a former "class mother" of mine at school. It occurred to me that I might find answers to a nagging question of why some seniors are a positive influence to others, and others are miserly, and only care about themselves. I suggested my writing biographies of "giving seniors", those who were unrecognized. At these offices it shouldn't be hard to find seniors who made a positive difference. She thought it was a great idea, and I was assigned to my first senior.

I called ahead to another local Office of Aging where Carl came daily. When entering, a booming voice rose up saying, "Well here comes Dorothy. I hear you will be interviewing me. I expect you to produce a Pulitzer Prize for your writing about me!" His attitude was sarcastic and he was challenging me. "What had I gotten myself into?" I worried. I thought of this burly man as Cantankerous Carl.

Carl was wheeled into an interview room for our interview. A "lap-robe" covered the stumps of his diabetic legs. He challenged me as

I turned on the tape recorder, asking why I wanted to know his life story, and I told him he was considered a leader here and I wanted to know more about him.

Well, that knowledge calmed him, and he led me through his life story. He told of how he had driven an ice cream delivery truck, and how he had supported his mother. He told of union meetings and his helping his friends and workers to negotiate their salaries. After his mother died, he lived with his sister and her children, who cared for him as he eventually developed serious diabetes and lost his legs. Currently he was driven to this Seniors' Day Care Center every day. He gradually loosened up with me, getting almost jolly in talking of his past in Brooklyn. He was never married, but instead supported his mother and he helped her raise his sisters.

Once the interview was over we went back into the main room and I stayed awhile and watched his interactions with the other seniors as they did crafts and had lunch. I watched his tenderness and helping one of the very senile ladies and his jokes and chiding of two of the elderly men. I understood why the director had chosen him to be honored.

The following week I returned with my finished story. It was only two pages long, but it was a tribute to Carl and his helping his mother and sisters and his leadership qualities with his union and his colleagues. My story pointed up his caring and help at the daycare center, even though he was wheel-chair bound. I lauded him as a leader and example for others.

Carl was stunned at what I had written. We presented him with a copy of my story and an honorary certificate. He was uncharacteristically quiet. The aides and the seniors all invited me back the next week.

The following week I again visited the center. He wanted to talk privately with me. He presented me with a "gift". It was a Gift Certificate for $5.00 for Friendly's Ice Cream Restaurant! (I hated taking his gift because I knew that he really couldn't afford it.) He told me that he had told his family that, at his death, he didn't want an obituary. He wanted the Life Story I wrote about him to be read! This "cantankerous" man was, underneath all, a bluff, dear, kind soul. When he was sent, in later weeks to a local nursing home, I visited him until a few months later when he died.

Carl's story inspired me to continue to write.

He Came Back

(The Past Interfering With the Present)

In an early "Musings" I wrote of Charlie, my first date, who played clarinet in the high school band. We were fourteen, and he took me to the movies. It was before WWII, and, in reflection, life seemed sweeter, more innocent. As naïve teenagers, our dates were simple, like going to the movies and the local amusement park, and each year he helped trim our family Christmas tree. When high school days were over, Charlie went into the army and later to a local college, and I went to college in New York City. We were involved in new pursuits and drifted apart.

Well, many years passed! After twenty-five years of teaching I was retired and had begun a second career in real estate. One morning, at my desk, I had a phone call from Charlie! However did he find me? He "happened to be in Putnam County," he told me, "and, could he take me to lunch?" By then my husband had died and my children were busy in their careers or in college so, intrigued by the call, I accepted. He said he would arrive around noontime.

I was red-faced and flustered when I hung up the phone, and Shari, the office secretary, asked me why I was upset. I told her about Charlie and the lunch date. I began to realize that I didn't know anything about Charlie after all those years. He could be a nice guy or an opportunist or a swinger or a bum! It was scary to think I had made a date with a stranger. In the early 1990's we didn't date through "match.com" meetings, and, now that I was in my 60's, I was no longer the cute teenager that Charlie knew. Realtors Sara and Joan, who were in the office with me, joined in the conversation, and asked me about the "old Charlie". I filled them in briefly.

Slowly the morning passed, and the girls kept teasing me, saying, you may be in for a date with another Robert Taylor or a Humphrey Bogart. On the other hand, he may be a weirdo with a big tattoo on his cheek. Who knew what all those years had done to him! After all, Charlie had been out in the world and could now be a sophisticate. By noon I was a nervous mess.

About noontime we saw a shadow pass the huge front window of the office and the door opened. In walked a man with shoulder length gray hair and a gold earring. His dark gray, wrinkled jacket had a tear near the right pocket. And he smelled! "Oh my God! Could this be Charlie?" I wondered. I heard Sara snicker as I stood up to greet this visitor. He was looking for another office and was asking directions! I fell back into my chair, relieved. Another ten minutes went by and another man opened the door. He was dressed in a white turtle-neck sweater, a tweed jacket, and nearly pressed pants, and he was even nice-looking! Of course, this was Charlie.

We went to a local diner and I heard all about Charlie's army career and his divorce and then he pulled out an old 4x6 black and white picture of me. It was tattered, but it was me at fourteen. I felt humbled by this keepsake and his memories of our past. He was still a nice man, a grown up version of the old Charlie, but too many years had gone by, and I heard the melancholy in his voice about his divorce from Terry, his sadness and yearning for her. He wanted to talk about her, and I wanted to hear it all. I realized that our past had been interfering in Charlie's life, and I told him to go to her and tell her he missed her and could they start over. Charlie and I parted that day with a hug and a promise to keep in touch. That Christmas I got a card from Florida. Charlie had found Terry and they were starting over. I was deeply touched that our teenage past had gotten in the way. Charlie saw that I wasn't the old girlfriend, the girl saxophonist. I had gray hair and wasn't the girl he remembered. His memories had stopped those many years ago.

We never know what the new day will bring, do we!

She Was Like a Rock

(Grandma)

As a young girl I'd sit on Grandma's bed and watch her uncoil and brush that beautiful white, wavy hair from its gigantic bun on top of her head. Her hair reached down to her waist. I can't remember her ever being young. She was only about five feet tall, a little stocky, but an energetic old lady with myriad wrinkles on her ever-smiling face. Grandma was a quiet, important presence in my life. She certainly had to be included in any musings.

She seemed to always be busy, cooking or tending to her petunias. I saw her only once a year because every summer my parents, my sister Betty, and I went back to The Bronx to visit each grandma for one week. In that one week I always felt Grandma B was kindly and a "good soul", but I never imagined how important she would be to me when I was older.

After college, and while working at Irvington House, a nursing home for recuperating rheumatic fever children, I met my future husband, Joe, also a "group leader" there. Because of religious conflicts, our engagement and marriage caused my parents to "write me off" and sever any relationship with me. But my Grandma B. and Aunt Dolly, stood by me. She was firm in her belief saying, "We either go up (pointing to Heaven), or we go down (pointing to the floor). What difference does it make how we worship God, as long as we are good people?"

And so, Grandma B. and Aunt Dolly helped me prepare for the wedding, and they celebrated with friends and Joe's family, my parents and sister not attending. It was sad for me, but still a wonderful occasion, with my little Grandma in the front in all the pictures. She was my father's mother, and he never spoke to her again because she stood by me. However, he did attend her funeral many years later.

When little Tommy was born, Grandma was right there, teaching me about my baby, how to wash him, tend for him, and, when I went back to summer school graduate courses, when Tommy was only six months old, Grandma invited Tommy and me to live with her while I commuted to Columbia University. By then she had to be in her seventies. Her kindness in those difficult times made my attendance at those courses possible, with my commuting almost an hour each way into New York City to attend classes, all the while doing reports and studying. By taking those courses I became qualified to teach school. Meanwhile, between his college years, my husband was working back at Irvington House.

Because of Grandma's help in my getting the needed courses, I was able to get a job teaching in New Hampshire and it gave us necessary living expenses. Little Tommy was well tended by a neighbor who had a baby girl, and so I could start my public school teaching, having had former experience with those rheumatic fever children.

After Joe's college years we moved back to New York and Grandma got to see my four children as they were born. She lived with Aunt Dolly, and was on a small pension, but she always brought a little box of animal crackers for each of the children when she visited. She taught me how to crochet and "tat", and she created beautiful handkerchiefs with delicately tatted edges. In those days people didn't have Kleenex tissues, but used handkerchiefs, often small works of art like those she worked on. Grandma died at 96 in a nursing home. The last time I visited her, she was in a rocking chair, tatting edges to making more handkerchiefs, still cheerful and smiling, never a cross word from her. When she died, I am sure she "went up", pointing to Heaven, welcomed by the angels as being one of them. She was like a rock.

I Didn't Do the Rhumba

(Or, Dating Dapper Danny)

When I was fourteen I edited the "*Mellonaire*" newspaper for Andrew W. Mellon Junior High School. Those were the days when radio was still young and advertisers had little birds chirping "Rinso-White, Rinso-White!" They also warned us, with someone's deep bass voice, about "B-O", to use a deodorant soap. I mention this because radio ads inspired me to make up a little "ditty" that I chanted over the school's public address system, hawking my "*Mellonaire*" newspaper for only 5 cents a copy.

I had just been taught the latest Rhumba dance steps by my best friend, Helen, who took dancing lessons every Saturday. I was hoping to be asked to the first dance of the school year, a "tea-dance" in the gym on Friday. (If you have read my previous stories you know about Charlie, the clarinet player in the school band who occasionally took me to the movies, but Charlie didn't want to learn to dance.)

By Wednesday I had given up hope for a date to the dance, when Danny, the very best looking ninth grader in the school, asked if I had a date, and if not he'd take me. He said he knew about me from my "*Mellonaire*" ditty over the P.A. I couldn't believe my luck! I had a dressy lavender-blue dress that was perfect to wear. To think Danny, a ninth grader, had asked me to my first dance!

He arrived early wearing a "jitterbug jacket", popular in the 40's. (The shoulders and the large lapels were light gray and the body of the jacket was a contrasting dark gray.) He wore a jaunty "pork-pie" hat. I thought I looked pretty grown-up with my lavender-blue dress, navy blue shoes with little heels, and silk stockings. He even gave me a pink flower corsage for my shoulder.

But, I never had a chance to show off my rhumba. I noticed in the car that Danny had brought a microphone and all kinds of chords and paraphernalia for a loud-speaker system. He hadn't asked me out to dance, he wanted me to announce the music he had recorded. He was the organizer of the dance, and I was to be his announcer! I felt like such a fool, thinking I was his date, and instead I was to be part of his act.

Danny had heard me over the P.A. system and thought I'd be the right one to promote his program. I think he probably had asked other girls who refused to be part of his act. I don't know that for sure, but, in any case, I felt used. But then, my pride told me that I'd make the best of it. Microphones didn't scare me. My dad had been making home-made records all year.

"Dapper Danny" didn't look so jaunty to me after that. Still handsome, but a phony! Well, in remembering that day, I think I did a pretty good job of announcing the music. I held back my tears and anger and tried to act like a professional. But I grew up a lot that day. I certainly learned to be more discriminating about dates. And after that, I learned lots of new Latin-American dance steps from Helen, and I brought boys from my class home for afternoon dance lessons. We would roll back the living room rug and dance to records that I bought with my allowance. Then, when more tea dances were announced, I had plenty of partners and a choice of dates. Grandma used to tell me to make lemons into lemonade. That's what I did.

My Best Friend Pat
(or "Lost Confidentiality")

When I was about twelve or thirteen, my best friend, besides Helen, was Pat. We would talk about life and tell our feelings and confide secrets to each other, giggling at things that happened at school. On nice fall and spring days we'd go to the high school tennis courts and roller skate, and rainy times we'd draw fashionable outfits for our paper dolls and trade them. Movies were on Saturdays, with a bag full of penny candy for the early serial of "Tom Mix" or "Flash Gordon". But everything changed when we were fourteen.

I cut off my pigtails and started wearing fitted sweaters and pleated skirts with brown and white saddle shoes and socks, and Pat got fat. I've written in other stories of my other girlfriend Helen teaching me to dance the Rhumba and then to "jitter-bug" (known as the Lindy Hop here in New York). Girls' parties began to include boys and dancing, and some even included the game of "Post Office" when a boy might kiss you on the cheek. But Pat was never invited.

I guess it was out of loneliness and feeling rejected, but Pat wanted to be included in the fun times and so she started to tell about the feelings, the longings, the thoughts that I had confided to her. She used the information about me to "get in good" with some of the girls. In looking back, I can't blame her, but, at the time, I felt betrayed. This experience made me wary for many many years of confiding in anyone. If my friend Pat, the one girl I trusted implicitly, would turn into such a deceitful person, could I trust anyone?

Besides telling my secrets, Pat became creative and said she could read palms. She started to be invited to parties because of this "talent" she had, and, she gradually felt better about herself as she was included more and more in high school parties, and, still heavy herself, she found a chunky boyfriend who, as a budding comedian, livened up parties with his "zingers" and compelling wit.

As the years went by, because of my experience with Pat I was cautious about sharing my feelings. Pat had destroyed the spontaneity I once had. When I eventually started story-telling and began to "muse" about life, I allowed myself to once again tell feelings. Recently, after the story "My First Date" was published, a friend said, "Dorothy, you are telling all about yourself." I answered, "Yes, why not?" She couldn't imagine letting people share her deep thoughts. You see, the experience with Pat had hurt me and for all those years I had stopped sharing true feelings. My relationships with girlfriends were casual and not close, because of this.

I tell this now because, half way through this "musing", I was talking to a young, stylish, sophisticated friend. She asked what my new story was about and I told her about Pat and how she had hurt me. She said, "And it's even worse now. People don't care about feelings, but only what they can do for themselves. Girls don't keep confidences. But then people put everything on Facebook anyway, not caring."

Is this what the world is coming to? Is trust and closeness and confiding in a special friend all lost? Can we no longer have close, confidential relationships? No wonder marriages are fleeting, relationships tenuous, loneliness is prevailing.

As I write these memories I am telling past secrets and experiences, but I find more and more readers coming to me confiding and telling me about their own past tenuous friendships, upsets and disappointments. Somehow they feel their hurts and hopes will be confidential with me. And they are.

Grandpa

(A Very Special Man)

Grandpa wasn't tall or good-looking, but he was spry and intelligent. When he married my grandmother, she was "disowned" because he was just the son of a tavern-owner, and her wealthy family owned a chocolate business. The only wedding gift that the parents gave the couple was a modest three-family house where the couple could live on the first floor and rent out the other two floors for a small income.

I guess Grandpa never made a lot of money in his life, but, when walking with him from their home on Poplar Street, neighbors waved from their porches or called "big hellos". I think he was rich with friends. His merry laugh and keen sense of humor made others happy to be with him.

To support the family, Grandpa worked as an architect's assistant in early 20th Century New York City, where land was being bought up and early mansions were being demolished, to be replaced by office buildings. Fancy furnishings and house decorations were sold at auction or just tossed out. Grandpa's boss let him take home elaborate drapery materials and knick knacks from rich houses. He also brought home several "coo-coo clocks" that all chimed on the hour, and fancy coin–banks. I particularly remember a William Tell Bank where an arrow shot coins into a cask, each time money was deposited.

At first, during our yearly visit, while the grownups talked, I loved playing with the elaborate doll house, discarded by a long-ago little girl. It had three floors, including an attic, and it was outfitted with wonderful miniature dolls and furniture.

I would eagerly anticipate Grandpa's finally taking me to his tiny backyard garden-haven. I looked forward to our reading the comics together. But Grandpa had to first exhibit to me his most beautiful flowers and newest plantings, keeping me waiting for the comics. He really was a tease! The twinkle in his eye told me he was purposely making me wait for our reading the "funny papers", as the comics were called.

Those old-fashioned houses were built close together, only about two feet between each one, and backyards were small. Glorious colors of all hues were in his magical garden that was clearly Grandpa's escape from the noise and clatter of the city and his five children. His wide grin showed me he enjoyed my appreciation of his lovely garden.

We'd finally sit on two little garden chairs, and then he'd "clear his throat" to read. I loved the misadventures of the "Katzenjammer Kids", a cartoon that was eventually renamed "The Captain and the Kids", and I laughed at Grandpa's reading about "Moon Mullins", with his derby hat, and his little brother, Kayo, who slept in a drawer, and I felt sorry for "Little Orphan Annie". I remember that Popeye's side-kick, Wimpy, was always eating a huge hamburger. We laughed over Major Hoople's "fez", and Dagwood Bumstead's multi-layered sandwiches and how he'd "turn-in" for a nap. Some of these cartoons eventually were made into "Big-Little Books".

Every year we'd visit one week with each of the grandparents, and, after we returned to Pittsburgh, Grandpa would roll together the month's comics into a package, and mail it to me so I could read them at home. It was our "connection", even though he was hundreds of miles away. He sent these "comic bundles" for years, until I became a teen and cut off my pigtails.

I loved that special togetherness with Grandpa. Those comics became a bridge between our generation-gap. How close two people can feel, enjoying beauty and sharing laughter and insights, even though decades apart in age! Our chuckling over those comics and sharing their lessons and messages, tied our thoughts. Young as I was, the pictures, the corny jokes and laughing together, made us "kindred spirits", even though we were probably fifty years apart in age. Thinking of Grandpa is a very special memory for me.

What's the Rush?

(Let Them Have a Childhood)

Children develop earlier today, physically becoming adolescents as much as two years earlier than in the past. This has been confirmed by doctors, and it is blamed on the hormones that are injected into meat and food. Even though children's bodies mature, their brains haven't fully developed, and so they are still young boys and girls mentally. "Pop Culture", the media, and the current climate of merchandising is capitalizing on this.

As early as first grade today, little seven and eight year olds have become the new market for provocative clothing. Advertisers show little girls' blouses with "drooping shoulders" showing underwear straps, and blouses are often transparent, revealing underclothes. Push-up bras are being advertised for the developing nine and ten-year old girls, and "thong" underwear or skimpy panties are promoted, especially in bathing suits. Sexy words are often printed on skinny leggings or tee-shirts. Recently psychologists evaluated thousands of today's children's clothing-products, finding that at least a quarter of the items being sold for young children have provocative sayings printed on them. Even baby's diapers have been seen with "sassy sayings" that parents think are so cute.

Why are we rushing our children into this "sophisticated" culture which is more daring and decadent? We're encouraging the wrong values. Why do we forget past values like goodness, honesty, dedication, and where is modesty? The dictionary says modesty is "reserve or propriety in speech, dress or behavior". What happened to our value system? I've written before about "everything hanging out" today, underwear, opinions, inner feelings. Do young children's clothes need to be so revealing? Shouldn't personal privacy be a value?

And why do clothes have those printed statements? T-shirts have become like Facebook, with provocative sayings. I guess the idea is to get attention. In some ways that can be good, knowing what others believe. We put ideas and feelings on the internet and social media like Facebook, never knowing who might be reading about us, parents, teachers, even future employers. The word "modesty" or even "privacy" doesn't seem important, until these opinions and ideas are read by the wrong people and used against us.

In past generations, children enjoyed their early years by playing simple games, learning to work and play with others. Their toys matched the simplicity of the immature intellect. Jump rope developed "timing". Hop Scotch taught balance, easy card games taught coordination and simple math. Coloring, sketching, and cutting-out honed coordination. We played "kick ball" and "hide and seek" and learned sportsmanship.

We had chores, working as a family. Some of us even earned small change doing odd jobs. We started small savings accounts, a little money deposited from earnings each week, learning thrift.

Today, after school, children are whisked away to dancing school classes, scout troupes, football/baseball teams. They don't learn "free play" enjoying "free time".

"What's the rush?" I ask. Families try to keep up with their friends and give the children "opportunities they never had". Let's let the little ones stay young longer, and enjoy this short but nourishing period of their lives. Growing up fast seems to satisfy parents, but the children are "short-changed" of a precious period in their lives. Parents let the children set the boundaries and make decisions because it is easier, to keep their children happy. But little ones aren't growing up happy without having learned positive values and self-control. Parents should be setting the boundaries when children are young and pliable. It doesn't get easier when they get to be teenagers. No wonder they can't be taught in the schools. It takes early self-discipline to learn and progress educationally.

What is the rush today?

Where Have the Old "Virtues" gone?

(The Media Is the Message)

I "muse" at how we educate our children. I remember special teachers who enriched my life, becoming life examples for me.

At eight years old I became aware of angels and nature's beauty because of my second grade teacher. Even though it was public school, she told us that "our guardian angels" keep track of what we do. She told us that they check whether we are good or bad, and our life's "good checks" get us into Heaven. This same teacher guided us in observing nature by having us find particular wild flowers and leaves of trees. We labeled our findings and ironed them into wax paper folds for a nature notebook.

This teacher also gave us copies of famous paintings that we put into notebooks, labeling these pages with titles and painters. Fifty years later I found a copy of Bartolome Muriello's "Boys with Grapes" and I had it mounted and framed, remembering her and my 2nd grade introduction to great art.

My third grade teacher read "A Child's Garden of Verses" to our class, and, years later, when I was a teacher, I introduced "I Had a Little Shadow" and the other poems to my first grade classes. I later learned that one of my students started writing her own poetry because of my readings.

My fifth grade teacher read a chapter of Kipling's "Mowgli" (from his <u>Jungle Book)</u> to us at the end of each class. Those stories inspired me to read well-written classic stories to elementary classes during "snack times".

In high school Latin class I was entranced by the wonders of ancient Greece and Rome. I began writing my first stories, my own imaginative "magical adventures" for the Latin teacher, who gave extra credit for any class writings. Because of that teacher, I dreamed of visiting Pompeii, and in the '90's finally did. Her love of the Roman and Greek myths inspired me to read children's versions many years later to my classes, hoping the stories would create interest in the classics.

In High School English class, I will never forget reading "A Man Without a Country", by Edward Everett Hale. This story inspired me with love for our wonderful country. That story should still be a requirement in high school. Not only is it beautiful writing, but it elicits pride in what we have and are.

Education requires three ingredients, a willing student, parents' cooperation, and an "inspired teacher". Most children today aren't exposed to good writing. They know Dr. Seuss's "Sam I Am" type poetry. They know the Disney's "watered-down" version of fairy tales that lack the morality lessons of the old fairy tales. Today's students know the rap words to sing along with their TV idols, and they can abbreviate words for Twitter. But can they write proper sentences and develop theses and proposals to pass freshman college English? Why do so many college freshmen have to take "remedial English"?

Why have we given in to forces who have taken "the virtues" out of our educational system, compassion, responsibility, friendship, courage, perseverance and faith? Plato said, "...tales which the young first hear should be models of virtuous thought." Does Dr. Seuss teach any values? Why have we allowed "rap music" to replace character education? Are parents aware of "rap words" and the insubordination, disrespect and violence instilled in those rhythmic cadences?

Where have the old "virtues" gone? No public school teacher today would dare talk about angels in class. Often today children are not taught manners and decency at home, and the media has become their prime education. Schools have become a second home, with parents too busy to discipline and guide, so schools have taken on the job of trying to teach the ABC's as well as "character education". Teaching toward the tests has become the rage, but it leaves little time for teaching how to live together. Somewhere, somehow we are losing our children. Somewhere, somehow our past values are fading. Unfortunately, "the media has become the message".

Being "Gaslighted"

(Light Influencing Emotions)

In the forties a movie, "Gaslight", starring Charles Boyer and Ingrid Bergman, showed a diabolical man manipulating his old fashioned "gas light" to gradually influence and "undermine" his poor unsuspecting wife. At that time, the expression "being gas-lighted" meant the slow, insistent, mind-bending use of light to weaken another's defenses. Light is an important aspect of our lives. Recently, our culture realized how the blinking of some fluorescent lights can upset the emotions. And those fluorescent lights were taken out of class rooms. I muse over our culture's use of light and its manifestations. Seeing one "light show" lately got my attention.

Years ago, I had a college friend who was majoring in physics and "light", and, at the time, I couldn't understand his obsession. In his basement he had flood lights, klieg lights, florescent lights and incandescent lights, all being tested for his theories. But now I realize that he was a man "before his time". He studied how light, and the use of it, could influence the senses. And today, the media, entertainers and advertisers are using light to influence people's emotions.

Now, the "Medium" is the message. In today's world, television and our entertainment industry is doing exactly what that man in

"Gaslight" did. It is slowly, insistently, mind-bending us, and especially our very susceptible, mesmerized youth.

In the early 1940's, a Frank Sinatra or Peggy Lee show would be on a huge stage, with foot lights, overhead stage lights, and spot lights. Peggy Lee might be "bathed" in a pale orchard light, delicately changing, depending on the mood of her song. As she sang out strongly, the light would morph into a brighter color, with orange and yellow hues, and then, changing into a blues' number, colors faded to suggest her emotions. The light centered only on her, and the audience would, almost reverently, be hushed and attentive.

In the mid-forties, girls gyrated in the aisles, paid by Sinatra's managers, and later, they screamed for "Ole Blue Eyes". In the fifties, girls shouted for Elvis Presley, the Beatles, and later "The Doors". In time wilder audiences experienced brighter spot lights, installed to hype the crowd's excitement. Run-ways were installed for the stars, to dance and prance over the audience, steaming them up, encouraging excitement. TV created "Happenings", using out-door arenas for more space, audience, and higher box-office proceeds.

Today these "Happenings" become "light shows", with flashing lights over the stage, the audience, the band, the performers. The show is shown overhead on numerous huge television screens, so that people seated a football-field length away can see all the action.

Of course, along with the brilliant lights flashing all around, the entertainers are loud, very loud. They usually hand-hold microphones and make faces and act-out as they sing/whine/mumble. And, to me, the music isn't usually pleasant. Instead, it is generally raucous, often raunchy, and, the music's words are seldom memorable.

What has developed is that young peoples' senses are being "challenged". The screaming music, the flashing lights, and the wild maniacal behavior of the entertainers-- are undermining sensitivities. Brash, crude behavior is accepted and applauded in our movies and TV shows. Even Queen Elizabeth, at her 60th Jubilee, feted Beatle Paul McCartney. Gentleness and manners seemed to have disappeared. Sadly, our culture has been "gas-lighted". I believe the current "junk culture" can't last.

Hope is on the horizon. There is still Tony Bennett singing the lovely old songs, and Rod Stewart recently made an album of "old standards". A young Diana Krall is currently appearing at Tanglewood, singing older more melodic songs as well as her own soft music. I believe the human spirit craves goodness and feeling, and this cycle will change.

Musical Opiates

(Dulling the Senses)

We had Elvis fans screaming in 1957, The Beatles' fans screaming in 1965, and in 1998 The Backstreet Boys were being screamed at and adulated by mostly teenage girls. In today's world, girls not only scream and swoon, but they spend hours on Twitter and Facebook talking about their current mania. History says that even in the 19th century young girls fought over locks of Franz Liszt's hair. Neuroscientests have been studying this behavior as well as brain waves and internal wiring.

Scientists at McGill University in Canada have discovered that when people hear familiar music there is a release of dopamine. This is the neurotransmitter that is involved in pleasure and addiction. This is the "rush" (or opiate) that the compulsive gambler feels, or the champion athlete experiences on winning. This is also involved when enjoying special candies and foods. Scientists in current research have witnessed MRI scans showing this process. This is interesting because they have found that during the teen years, musical and critical tastes appear to become part of the brain's internal wiring. They tell us that these are formative years, with neural pathways solidifying and some are even "pruned away". Adult's nostalgia comes from their past teenage wiring and neural paths. The recording industry has becoming expert in exploiting this.

We used to consider this "romantic mania" innocent and a harmless stage in growing up. Adolescent girls are particularly susceptible, just waking up to sexual feelings. We thought that having a "crush" on a celebrity is a safe way to express these new feelings. In the past, some girls believed they loved the young Shaun Cassidy or, in today's world, the current boyish- looking Justin Bieber. The popular songs play on teenage fantasies, like the new song "Boyfriend", saying, "If I was your boyfriend I'd never let you go." A romantic girl would believe he is talking to her. Girls play videos of their heroes over and over, reinforcing their imagined love. Boys identify with athletes and often emulate them, even as some grown men identify with specific teams and sports, still imagining their youth.

Psychologists now feel this isn't healthy behavior. These young people are living in a fantasy world and later they have a difficult time adjusting to the real world and real boyfriends, or the fact that they are not those sports individuals. The media encourages a fantasy world from the tiniest tots who identify with princesses and princes. Storybooks and movies continue this escaping into a never-never land. Weddings have gotten more and more ornate, some families mortgaging their homes to pay for this fairy-land experience, only to have the couple divorce in a few months, not having the wonderland they expected from marriage.

But there is more to be considered. Adolescence is the time in development when the brain needs the stimulation of sensitivity toward culture, fine and beautiful melodies, appreciation of the arts. Staying at a "jungle beat" level, with crassness of ideas without the humanities or a concern of mankind and culture, is handicapping our youth. While young people's brains are viable and capable of assimilating the finer aspects of life, we limit their appreciation of beauty by letting the wrong "happenings" to influence our youth.

I believe there are changes coming. I notice that more people are worried about our culture. I read of the new generation thinking this over, soberly realizing that these concerns need to be addressed. I see young peoples' dramatic groups and art galleries opening. All around I feel a stirring of educated people who want to join young people in the arts. There is a renewal in the history of our nation and the ideals that we used to foster. This knowledge of the development of the critical brain areas and the formation of ideas and standards can redirect our educators and parents toward helping young people to enjoy a better quality of life, and with it, higher ideals. We must waken the senses of our youth to the beautiful, creative and humane world we know.

It's Confirmed That "Big Brother" Is Watching
("Brave New World")

A friend recently remarked, "What difference does it really make if government, advertisers, social media know all about me? So what if my Email, my phone, my "Smart Phone" are being tapped?" At first, I thought, it really doesn't matter. I'm not a spy or doing anything illegal. I tell my readers all about my past, my thoughts and opinions anyway. Why should I care about the "data-base" that is set up "somewhere out there", about me?

I reflected about the time when I was a psychology major at college. World War II was over and our classes discussed the gigantic propaganda machine the Germans had, and how the people had been suckered into the philosophy and ideas of Hitler, how they were convinced of the statements that were being spewed out to influence the people. They went along with his ideas, almost like lemmings that blindly follow their leaders, even to death. At that time, psychology was a fairly new "major" in college, interested in social values and trends, abnormal capabilities and problems, and the NEW advertising empires that were being built up. The statistics involved with studying trends and peoples' habits became a major part of the advertising world.

We studied the advertising propaganda devices that the Germans used, in order to be so successful. We discussed their powerful effects on the public, and we saw how advertising in our country would eventually become a huge industry. (The "Mad Men" TV shows of today mirror how advertising blossomed here after the war.)

But today we learn that the National Security Agency has been tracking the phone calls and online communications of millions of our people. And, even aware that our identity and activities are no longer secret, we have accepted this. We have allowed credit card retailers to store our information. We use the charge card they gave us, seemingly convenient, even though all of our purchases go into their data base and eventually into the master file of collected data about our private lives. We show our "Wellness Card" at the drug store, in order to get the 10% or so discount on purchases, not even thinking that all those personal products we buy tell others information about our health and private life. We use our library cards that tally all the titles and types of books we borrow. We send donations to personal interest groups, revealing our religions and political affiliations. They, in turn, sell our names and information about us to other groups for future dunning. All of this is in the data system about us.

Facebook and Twitter are popular with those who want to reach out to others easily, but do they realize that the thoughts, movements, indiscretions that are cited on line are being tallied and viewed, not only by friends, but sometimes by future employers, government agencies and not always friendly surveillance agents.

What about all those dating services? Often the pictures are dated and the information stated is exaggerated or untrue, but those using the services are feeding information that goes into the data bank about them. And anyone borrowing their computer is adding to that data.

What about a precocious teenager who played a raunchy game or accessed a questionable program on your computer when you weren't looking? Or a family member who is trying to get a loan and is giving out personal information, using your computer? This is added to your record.

Accountants and bankers have people send private information on line. It's no longer private now though. Were we really aware of this?

It has become almost impossible to live without Email or cell-phones, but all the information is no longer private. Maybe we should stop entering contests on Email, or answering polls to win a credit card. We should be more diligent as to what information we have been freely giving out.

Does it make a difference? I personally have had my computer hacked and have been the object of scams several times in just the last three years. I am going to be more circumspect now with any credit cards I use or what information I give out on Facebook or even on my telephone. Shouldn't you do this too? "Big Brother" is watching.

Correction for "Big Brother Watching" Column

(Accuracy is Important When Writing)

In my September 3, 2013 column, "Big Brother Is Watching" I wrote, "We use our library cards that tally all the titles and types of books we borrow." I went on to say that these records could be used by groups that want information about us for future advertising.

When I researched for this "Big Brother" article, I used information from **The New York Times** for my column. A "Friend" of the Mahopac Library System called me to correct this. I then contacted the library director who was happy to give me the proper information so I could correct my article and inform readers.

I was happy to learn that there is a New York State law regarding Library Card Users' Privacy:

> "Confidentiality of Library Records: The Library protects the privacy and confidentiality of its patrons and staff as required by state and federal law. Confidential library records, whether those records are in print, film, magnetic tape, electronic, or some other format still to be developed, shall not be released or made available to a federal agent, law enforcement officer, or other person unless a court order in proper form has been entered by a court of

competent jurisdiction after a showing of good cause by the law enforcement agency or person seeking the records….."

This is comforting information, and I appreciate the help of the Mahopac Library Director in sharing it with me. Libraries have always been my sources of information, my havens for good reading and relaxation, and the best and finest institutions in any area.

"Selfies", the Word of the Year

(Today's Narcissism)

Yes, you read it correctly, "selfies" is the current "word of the year", according to actor, director, and writer James Franco. When I read this in *The New York Times*, "Arts and Leisure Section", 12/29/13, I was fascinated by what the article was talking about. I realize that our culture, and particularly our young people, have become more and more self-absorbed. We used to call it "conceited". The word "narcissism" comes to mind.

The words "narcissism" and the term "narcissistic" come from the Greek myth of Narcissus, a handsome Greek youth who fell in love with his own reflection in a pool of water. This myth has evolved today into the meaning and the term narcissistic, to mean, "the admiration of one's own physical self, or arrogant pride". Psychological scores of residents of the United States have detected an increase in narcissism since the year 2000 and this is linked by psychologists, to the increase of "social networking" today, Facebook, the Media, "Stardom".

But why do I care about all of this? Because I believe that parents are a primary cause of this self-focus. I taught the primary grades for over twenty-five years, and I saw parents coddling their children. Some of my students' parents, in their first "school orientation meeting" protested homework for first grade children. I explained that fifteen to twenty minutes of homework each evening for first graders was for practicing what had been taught during the school day so that, on the following day, the class could go onto another step in learning. Also, I believed that each child should experience the discipline of doing what was directed. In order to progress in learning the "A, B, C's", practice was needed, and the discipline of putting aside that short period of time each day for practice was equally important.

In teaching the parents the importance of homework, I also did my part by seeing that the work I assigned was checked each day, not an easy job with a large class. In time, my classes' parents usually worked with me, finding real progress and positive results in learning.

But homework is just a small piece of this coddling. Parents today are suddenly learning that their children aren't as brilliant as they thought they were. There is a modern cult of "self-esteem", a worry that their children can't stand being challenged, that it might hurt egos. There is the idea that tougher instruction might discourage children from enjoying school. Maybe it is too stressful, not fun. Maybe school is too hard.

But, isn't it true that life isn't always easy? Isn't it true that sometimes stress and strain must be employed to go to further steps in learning and achievement? Shouldn't children, even young children, learn that hard work can accomplish things? We have resorted to insulating our children from "blows" to their egos. We used to award trophies to victors, and now they go to everyone, to be sure no one is left out.

But, back to "selfies". The author of the article in *The New York Times* prides himself in being the "Selfie King", posting the most "likes" from followers in Facebook. He claims that "a well-stocked collection of selfies gets attention". And attention is "the name of the game" in social net-working.

We may distain and sneer at disgusting behavior in our celebrities, but who is named "Star of the Year" but the most narcissistic, outrageous, entertainer. You can win the Heisman Trophy by being a "top gladiator" athlete, even though your social behavior is deplorable and often even criminal. We reward the selfies, the narcissists, because they are the money-makers, and isn't all that money the proof that they are the BEST! Sadly, our society's yardstick is money, not decency, not kindness, not intelligence, not real human values.

Guns, Movies, and Video Games,
(Letter to the Editor)

The recent massacre of children has affected us all and demands we look at what has been affecting our culture and our youth. My deep concern is over the insidious, creeping, cultural changes we have allowed. It's like a nasty infection, gradually eating away the goodness and decency we want for our society and coming generations.

We can eliminate the guns, but it's the disrespect for one another that has been permeating our culture and that has been encouraging this creeping violence. How many years have we seen the emergence of more and more violence in our movies, our comics, our cartoons, our TV, and, more recently, our video games! It used to be that "jazzy sneakers" connoted the adolescent who is "with it", who is "cool"! But now, today's youth and those who are "with it" must have the latest video games.

How many parents know the content of the video game their child is obsessed with? Do they know what the game contains that their child wants, the game that all the popular kids own, the game that makes him part of the crowd? Unlike a violent TV show, the video game involves actually using the hands, the brain, the feelings and emotions of the watching participant. The watcher feels he is actually part of the spectacle. He participates in the story. In a recent video game called "Call of Duty-Black Ops" the player has a choice of weapons to kill hundreds of people. This is approved for children twelve and over by the "Common Sense Media" group!

At first it was the educators and now it's the scientists who tell us what the games do, for and to our children. We thought of Nintendo games as a harmless activity, new games for children. But now, new studies tell us that these intense video games can actually take over the brain of the player. They encourage short attention spans and a high level of stimulation. The players are captivated, being part of the action. They take part in the actions, maybe even the cruelty. Many of the video "games" have women being maltreated by men. Others show greediness and violent pain inflicted. Who can watch people being degraded, cruel punishments, sadistic rituals, over and over and not ultimately be affected? And too often it isn't the mature adult player participating in the "game". It's a young person who is just beginning to establish his own value system and beginning to think of his future role in life.

While engaged in viewing these "games", the participants are given unhealthy powers to inflict harm and even torture. And worse, these "games" involve all the senses, the visual, audio, and even the tactile. They could change the viewers' minds and behaviors. The developing maturity of the adolescent can be twisted and deeply influenced by the brain's being taken over.

That twisted sense of power and meaning of life can easily possess a sensitive youth's brain. Why aren't we looking at these devious, insidious creeping obsessions in our society? We give movies'

101

numbers so that parents are aware of their content. According to a salesperson I recently interviewed, an adult has to show identification when buying these violent videos. But parents and adults are buying them for the young people. Do today's parents know what is being cultivated into their growing, developing child's mind? Of course the youth with a strong self-image and strong set of values can overcome this poison. But what of the others?

A recent *New York Times Magazine* (September 2010) has a hopeful article about how recently some educators are putting to use the power of such games, and they are formulating educational material using the repetitious, audio/tactile benefits of video games to teach. This could be excellent for this generation of young people who are so advanced in the new technical culture. It would be a valuable teaching aid if used the right way. This is my hope for the future.

But, meanwhile, let's look more carefully at what values we are cultivating with ubiquitous video games!

Love For Our Country

(Lost Patriotism)

In my "Musings" column 12/04/13, I mistakenly named Sir Walter Scott the author of "The Man Without a Country". The author was Edward Everett Hale. I was too hasty in writing my thoughts about current virtues and values. When I write I must check every fact. (Sometimes I'm impatient, anxious to get my thoughts on paper.) The story "The Man Without a Country" is about fictional Philip Nolan, an Army Lieutenant, an accomplice to treasonous Aaron Burr. At his trial he said, "I wish I may never hear of the United States again!" The judge granted his wish and forced him to travel naval ships "on the high seas" the rest of his life. No one was to mention the United States to him again, and he was to get no news from home.

Through the years he begged the ship's sailors to tell him about the United States, and, not until his death did he hear about the country's changes. He missed the United States dearly, and had draped the flag that he remembered over a picture of George Washington, and he had drawn an outdated map of the country with its former territories that had become states. He asked to be buried at sea. He wanted his "death-epitaph" to state, "In memory of Philip Nolan, Lieutenant in the Army of the United States. He loved his country as no other man has loved her; but no man deserved less at her hands."

During discussions of this story, our class also memorized "Innominatus (Patriotism)" by Sir Walter Scott, causing me to confuse the authors in my recent column. That wonderful poem begins:

> "Breathes there the man with soul so dead,
> Who never to himself hath said,
> This is my own my native land!..."

Please look up this entire poem if you are interested in a heart-rending, beautiful classic piece. I still get teary-eyed reading it and thinking of Philip Nolan in Hale's story. I wish today's readers and students could have the same renewal of patriotism that I feel each time I read these pieces.

Recently, Edward Snowden has been called "The Man Without a Country". Snowden has become today's embodiment of Philip Nolan, from that 150-year-old story. Snowden recently worked at our government's National Security Agency, and was identified as the source for secret reports that he revealed about our country's intelligence programs. He sees himself as a loyalist to human rights, putting "information openness" above his U.S. nationality. His actions have opened up areas of this country's national security. Snowden left our country, taking secret intelligence information with him.

And, more shocking, since 2011, dozens of our young men, having been lured online in English by jihadists, have gone to Syria to join Al Qaeda. (See page A16, *The New York Times International*,

104

12/05/13.) Our American intelligence officials warn that these men, aged 18 to 30, "could create new terrorist threats when they return home!" The *Times* article tells of the Global Fund for Community Engagement and Resilience (a $200 million fund), that is attempting to "...educate young people about the dangers of violent extremist ideologies." The group is awarding grants to educate young people and warn them about Al Qaeda. Our State Department officials say that Tamerlan and Dzhokhar Tsarnaev used information from Al Qaeda's online magazine, *Inspire*, to fashion the pressure-cooker bombs used in the Boston Marathon attack. The White House and our FBI and CIA agencies are noticing Al Qaeda's appeal to some of our youth.

Where are the educators and patriotic forces that inspire our young people? This simple story about a man who regretted losing his country has lived with me all these years. My generation deeply loves America. Today, thousands of our young people have given their lives to volunteer and serve in our armed forces, showing a love of our country. What is happening today to lose the others to betray our country? Why are we losing them?

Today's Music Giants

(Grammy Awards)

The latest Grammy Awards have me concerned about the influence of today's music on our youth. I have said before that "the media is the message" and it has unfortunately come true. Although beautiful dance, music, and concerts have been available in our culture, the crude side of the "music industry" has captivated the senses and mentalities of the majority and brought our tastes down to primitive levels.

In my book "Musings" I wrote of studies that show what tremendous forces color and light can be to the brain, especially when we attend a "happening". Some producers are concerned with true sensual beauty and the affects can be "soul-satisfying", calming, relaxing, memorable. But unfortunately, today the tendency is to promote the outrageous, especially the provocative. Some of our young "stars" like Miley and Justin seek negative publicity in their personal lives, and their antics keep their names in the newspaper, and the more surprising and outrageous they are, the more publicity they get, and with publicity they get larger audiences and money. Tickets for their shows go for over $250 for the good seats! Money is fame today. I have written before about our sports' gladiators who can do no wrong. The more anti-social their behavior, the more publicity, the more money. The same can be said for the rest of the entertainment industry and its questionable awards.

Elvis died over thirty-six years ago, but he is still remembered, and recently nearly 20,000 fans held a candlelight vigil outside the gates of Graceland. His career lasted twenty-three years, starting as a country blues singer, then a hip-swiveling rocker, a movie star, a gospel singer, a soul balladeer, a Las Vegas headliner, to finally a pill-dependent recluse. To thousands, he is still a star. One attendee at a recent Elvis Week in Memphis said he has been attending Elvis concerts for fifteen years. He said Elvis is "a connection to a simpler, gentler time."

But why do I bring him up? Because he has become even bigger in time. The sexuality in his early performances was at first "covered up" in the Ed Sullivan shows, and then was gradually promoted as his agents saw it made money. His drug-dependency was a model for our youth. And since then, bumps and grinds have become popular and many have imitated him and have enhanced sexuality in their acts. And now, today, the opening song and dance in the Grammys by Beyonce', and the dubious amorous double-and-single-entendre's the songs and dancing throughout the show created, showed intolerable vulgarity. The Grammy's Award show was given large advertising spreads as the latest "blast" for our "musical giants".

And, to top the whole program off, thirty-three gay and straight couples were married by, of all people, Queen Latifah, deputized by Los Angeles County (as written by *The New York Times*, January 27, 2014). Outrageous! I was shocked by this. What more can these "entertainers" do to defile conventional thinking and mores! What used to be back-room and burlesque entertainment is now everywhere. And we wonder what is poisoning our children! Everywhere, in all the media, we see nakedness, sexuality, with old-fashioned mores and modes of conduct being ignored, and we are elevating pornography, calling it creative. Am I the only one disgusted with the pollution in our culture? Now drugs are to be legalized. As though our youth has not been "dumbed down enough" by our current culture!

We should be celebrating the good kids, the hard-workers, the heroes all around us who defy this vulgar down-slide of our culture. Parents shake their heads, knowing their daughters are out sitting on the bar stools, and they worry about their boys who can't hold jobs and refuse more education to rise above the masses. Have you listened to the words of "rap music"? Have you seen the seductive performances of our "music stars"? And have you encouraged and lauded the brave souls who dare to remain decent with moral standards?

Poisoning Our Children

(With Pop Culture)

Recently our nation was nervous about possible war, anxiously tuned in to the impassioned speech of Secretary of State, John Kerry, who enlightened us with the intelligence report saying there was substantial evidence of chemical weapons being used by Syria in the Damascus suburbs. Prior to his speech, we had been appalled and horrified by seeing TV scenes of terrified children being taken to be killed, and by seeing dead children's bodies laid out on the ground. We were told that more than 1,400 Syrians were now dead, 429 of them children. His speech was hoping to justify a US military strike on Syria. How could they poison their children?

During the same time period, news stations showed us outrageous scenes from the August MTV Video Music Award Show. Particularly disgusting was the sexually charged dancing and freaky performance of Miley Cyrus, the former Hannah Montana, a Disney child star. They said her dancing was "twerking", a new word now in the dictionary. This involved lewd dancing, including "rump shaking", and miming coitus, while she was wearing a nude-colored bikini. And in the past, Hannah Montana was a model for our young girls!

Compounding this sexually suggestive performance was the fact that the Parents Television Council, with Miley's father on the advisory board, rated this program appropriate for kids as young as fourteen. They tell us that the mission of this group is to "protect children from graphic and gratuitous programming and to restore responsibility to the entertainment industry". This display copied many rap and hip-hop dancing techniques. It was the "pop" culture exemplified.

Do you see what is happening? While the Syrians are poisoning their children with chemical ingredients, we are standing by as the media and entertainment industry is poisoning our children with rap, hip-hop, and "twerking". We are allowing our children to become part of the "trendy culture" of lewdness, the appropriation of questionable cultural rap-type dancing, and being immersed in anti-woman violent songs and suggestive dancing.

Our young people go by the hundreds, to these "happenings", to rap and hip-hop concerts, completely entranced by the mind-blasting music and swayed by the creative lighting and visual effects. We see them on TV at these concerts, totally mesmerized by the "music", the lighting, the rhymic undulations of the performers. Anything goes, including sexual lyrics, often degrading women, wearing suggestive costumes, performing lewd dancing! The hundreds in the audiences can be seen, gyrating almost as one to the outrageous! Often drugs are involved. Our youth are mesmerized by these hours they spend at the "concerts", when their bodies are totally taken over.

These sessions are poisoning our children! Allowing these gatherings, we are not being good parents and grandparents. These influences are weakening our young peoples' determination to be good, to be responsible citizens. Their minds are systematically

110

being infected. They want to be liked, to be part of the system. They want to be accepted in the groups who are already weakened and infected. Those with a low self-image are especially susceptible to these "forbidden fruits".

Years ago, when I was a teacher, I found using rhythm and rhyme helped the little ones to learn their alphabets, their times-tables. By constant repetition and chanting, the slowest student learned. When all the senses are involved, similar to a "happening", the dramatic lighting, the sounds, the rhythms, the force of the crowd, the sexual messages are absorbed and learned.

Years ago it was said, "The medium is the message." And it is. We are letting our young people become corrupted, poisoned. We don't need to use chemical substances. Our culture is much more subtle. We allow corruption and evil in the media to overcome the senses. There's an absence of the old morals. We see less respect

for parents, the old, and the infirm. Surrounded by these low moral standards, an impressionable young person with little or no parental guidance who wants to be accepted will often "act out", in order to fit in with the group. How hard it must be for young people today to be good with what surrounds them! Can't we responsible adults do something about this? Where are the parents? Where did the sweet, young, Hannah Montana go?

Where Is Love?

(Relationships with Benefits)

I am concerned about where our culture is going when I read today's statistics that say marriage is being postponed, on average, to about twenty-nine years old for men and twenty-seven for women, if they even get married. Less and less of our young people are marrying, opting instead to "hook up" and have "relationships with benefits". (For the older, "uneducated generation", that means, relationships that include sex.)

Aside from the immorality, this desensitizes young people to what real love is, and creates an emotional vulnerability. Popular TV shows and current movies tout sexual activities as being the sophisticated way to be popular. From early teens, young people are captivated by matinee idols who show narcissism and sexuality. The "stars" perform at huge "happenings", with thousands attending. These shows use all the latest "lighting experiences", mesmerizing attendees with moving lights and special effects that dun the senses and influence the emotions. The excessive sound-volumes and audience's screaming at these shows overwhelm the senses.

Besides the auditory and sensory immersion, the performers gyrate, undulate, "twerk", in suggestive costumes, singing and rapping sexual lyrics. The peer pressure alone, with all the audience screaming and moving, immerses the easily suggestible young people.

But I have written before about these events and their dangers for our youth. We now have "easy available sex" everywhere and a fast moving culture, with quick "hook-ups" for dates and, by trolling the computer, available dates for all. And, easily available pills and condoms can prevent pregnancy.

The old-fashioned courting and flirting are no longer the fashion. Relationships often begin at parties and bars, and all ages are finding available dates and easy "hook-ups". Girls' scanty outfits with skirts half-way up the thighs and low-cut bodices are provocative, and the heavy make-up with dark eye-liner are their attempts at being seductive.

But with all of the easy dating, this generation is clueless about romantic intimacy. The brazenness modeled in the media and movies shows an emotional emptiness. The "stars" are our models and show sexiness as being fashionable.

This all leads to emotional emptiness. Quick, easy sex drains feeling, according to psychological reports. Our youth are becoming desensitized and experience "emotional corrosion" according to the studies. Hormones are released during orgasms, but real intimacy isn't attained. In the book "Love and Survival", Dr. Dean Ornish states, "I am not aware of any other factor in medicine that has a greater impact on our survival than the healing power of real love and intimacy." But too often people don't know how to show or feel real love, to discern between love and infatuation. They lack interpersonal skills and how to know and feel real love versus submitting themselves to cheap relationships with "benefits". It's no wonder the divorce rate is 40% to 50% today.

Young people today think of sexual activities as "past-times", without the intimacy and real personal involvement. Then, if there is a pregnancy, the males walk away, and the girls are left wondering why they have the final responsibility of a child. "Educated girls", who avoid pregnancy, often are saying they may have children, someday, but not now.

It truly is a different culture, with different values, different standards. Unfortunately, this generation often doesn't recognize real love, real intimacy. The quick infatuations are disappointing and even debilitating. Despondency so often occurs, possibly with resorting to the ever present drugs. And we wonder why our youth are depressed! Why they often turn to the numbing of drugs. If parents aren't children's examples of real love in their relationships, and churches aren't reaching our youth, how do our young people experience and know how to love?

Hope on the Horizon

(Old-Fashioned Values)

Our sportsmen are our heroes, today's gladiators. Tens of thousands crowd into stadiums witnessing every sport. Crowds cheer, each person attending internalizes the game, and if his team wins, he feels that he wins too. At the "afterward parties" shouts are heard "We won!" No matter what scandals are attached to the team or to their favorite players! No matter the sport, football, baseball, college sports, rugby, golf. The computer's Wikipedia states that major sports scandals are involved in every sport.

You've read of the sexual indiscretions, the fake injuries, the match fixing, the doping scandals of our sports' heroes. Yet, if a player makes the right moves on the field, he can win a prestigious trophy such as the Heisman Trophy, regardless of his lack of character. What does such a trophy indicate? Prowess on the field, but certainly not a person to be admired.

In our entertainment world, thousands pay homage and plenty of money to view "celebrities", and worship in their presence. Our young people attend "happenings" where obscenities, nakedness, ear-splitting, mind-wrenching sounds, activate bodies with those on stage. The multi-hued moving lights mesmerize, and the audience claps and moves almost as one, to the rhythms.

And then there is Miley Cyrus, the former Disney "Hannah Montana", who used to be a teen-age model for young girls, and, at twenty-one, has decided to be a porno-queen, performing this August at the MTV Music Awards at the Barclays Center in Brooklyn. A former story of mine told of my disgust at her decision to change her image for the fame and money her "rump-shaking" and "twerking" has brought her. But now she is a "star" because of her disregard of all decency. Our young people's money has made her a so-called top performer. I heard recently that a ticket to her performance was $250! This girl I spoke to, and her boyfriend, paid $500 for the two seats!

Just as we reward the sports figures, despite their sometimes scandalous behavior, we have foolishly made Miley a prominent cultural symbol.

But I am not just writing this to be negative. There is hope out there.

The Jet's Wide Receiver, David Nelson, signed in October, is quoted as saying, "Football is what I do. It's not who I am." He and his two brothers have traveled to Haiti seven times in the process of obtaining legal guardianship over twenty-two children in Haiti. These were abandoned children. He saw that they weren't interested in money or candy. David said, "They just want me to hold them, sing them a song, or play soccer with them." He is starting a non-profit organization "I'mME", that is to help abandoned children. Why isn't his story a front-page headline?

And also, another story caught my attention. Recently two Brewster High School juniors organized an "Annual Day of Service", where love, kindness and assistance highlighted the day.

They conceived the idea with the first anniversary of the Newtown Massacre in Connecticut. They organized high school students to give craft activities and story-telling to the elementary students, focusing on kindness and compassion toward others. Students from the middle-school joined in with activities as did others from all over the school district. These are youth we can be proud of.

It is our dollars running this, our denying the values we used to believe in. We used to have "watch dogs" like the Hayes Office back in the 1930's and '40's who saw that obscenities and indiscretions were kept out of our Hollywood Movies. But this was challenged and our radical courts removed their influence. After that, anything could, and did, creep in. We have no watch dogs except our parents and concerned adults today.

My hope is in the David Nelsons and the young Brewster High free-thinkers. They are doing what they believe in. Somehow their goodness and foresightedness will overcome. Someone has taught them well. They are our true heroes.

"Relating" to My Readers

(Feedback From Readers)

Friends ask me about readers' responses to my "Musings". I love hearing from readers and seeing them in the local stores or at meetings, hearing about the columns that they can "relate" to, and when I should follow up on subjects.

When I first started writing these columns in May 2010, I explained where the word "musing" came from. Some of you never read those old columns, which are now included in my book "Musings", published in July 2012, by Amazon (available at Amazon.com and Kindle). The dictionary defines musings as (adj.) "absorbed in thought, abstracted", and (noun) "contemplation, meditation". I often wake up around 4:00 am with a new thought or idea to develop into a "Musings" column. I've come to realize that the more I dig back into the past with memories, the more the connections come back to me. I tell others to do the same. Of course, some of those memories are ones we want to forget, but, by bringing them up we can see how we overcame or lived through them. Actually it can be therapeutic, remembering how we got through the tough times.

My stories are all true. Musing of them and writing them now, in my eighties, has been such pleasure for me. I recommend this to you all, if only for your family to really know the person you are and have been. Your backgrounds and feelings should be written and "gifted" to your families as part of their heritages.

I got "feedback" from some stories more than others. In my published book "Musings", "The Secret Life of Mary", "An Abused Little Girl", and "The Magic of Touch" specially elicited attention. Readers were touched and related to these. Strangers saw me and gave me hugs, encouraging me to continue my writing. To think that what I remembered was important to others inspired me to go on and write more.

My "Weenies (A Young Bride's Story)" had readers telling me of their adventures in New Hampshire. "Wherever Did You Go, Ellen?" has haunted me and has "touched" several readers. "From Silver Slippers to House Slippers" brought comments in agreement because of their own leg and foot tortures from some shoes. Several of my past students got in touch with me because of their reading my stories of the puppet shows we produced in my elementary school classes. And, of course, my story of "Where's Rusty?", a beautiful Irish Setter, had dog-lovers calling me.

But most calls and Emails' comments were about my recently published story, "Poisoning Our Children" (With Pop Culture Images). (*The Putnam Times/Press* 9/18/13) It was a long column, longer than usual, as I unloaded my distaste, my disgust, my concern, for what is corrupting today's youth. Miley Cyrus, the Disney-backed sweet young character, Hannah Montana, a model for our young girls, has grown up to the old age of about twenty-one to become a sexually charged new image and example for our girls. Her raunchy moves and what she calls "twerking" has given her the publicity and money she wanted, and she bragged to Matt

Lauer on the "Today Show" that "it's as we planned" and "a month later and we're still talking about it!" She even talks of loving marijuana. Her new video shows her swinging naked on a wrecking ball.

Wouldn't it be ironic and "poetic justice" if all her efforts for publicity and notoriety contributed to her being boycotted, snubbed, ignored by the public. If only "Women's Libbers", PTA groups, religious groups, just plain **concerned** parents, "took a stand" and used her as their "Decadent Poster Loser of the Year". Too bad I'm so old and fragile or I could lead a concerned parent group in a boycott, a rejection of her deliberate campaign to infect our youth into decadence! Wasn't there a song once called "Send in the Clowns". And the words said, "...don't bother, they're here."

Brain Changes with Love

(Love Lessons Can Make a Deep Impression)

Neurobiologists are studying the brain, now that we have machines for imaging. One of the great discoveries in our era has found that the brain is constantly rewiring itself. In a past "Musings" ("Being Gaslighted", published 03/29/12) I told of how light, all kinds, including "light shows", can influence the senses. I've also written about music being powerfully "hard-wired" into our brains ("Music and the Senses", 08/04/10) with Alzheimer's patients beating time and dancing to their past memorable music, even though all other past memories seem to be forgotten.

In another of my past stories, ("A New Beginning", 03/23/11) I cited the studies of Dr. Oliver Sacks ("The Mind's Eye", publisher Knopf) who specializes in afflictions of the brain. He found that the parts of the brain damaged in a stroke or by old age can "reshape themselves by the process of compensation". His belief is that people can make up their lost ability with new emotional adjustments such as developing other ways of doing things and learning new strengths. He believes that the part of the brain that once processed these lost abilities does not atrophy, but reallocates for another use. I personally have felt this with my lost hearing abilities, now reallocated into my experiencing past memories and so writing of them.

And so, it isn't surprising that the neuroimaging of the brain shows baby's brains registering the mother's voice, face, and expressions of love. And even more fascinating is the fact that, as we mature, find friendships, have affairs, find romantic love and possibly a soul mate, the brain becomes reshaped with each new experience. Drs. Daniel J. Siegel (a neuroscientist) and Allan N. Schore, both of the University of California, Los Angeles, have conducted conferences on the brain and what they call "supportive relationships". They find that "loving relationships significantly alter the brain".

When relating to a friend we look at the world through another's eyes. Often we take on their habits, try new foods and enjoy new experiences with them. We meet their friends, finding new relationships. All of this "revamps" the brain. When becoming a "couple" we extend ourselves to include the other person, becoming like the loved one, learning to enjoy their pleasures.

But, scientists caution, the same areas of the brain that register physical pain are active if the relationship turns into rejection, our whole body feels the pain. The nerve fibers give messages that register rejection and even feel physical assault. Loss of a loved one can trigger the same distress as a stomachache or even a fractured limb. But, just the physical touch of a loving person or even a loving pet can lower the neural pain response in the brain. Because a basic need is to love and be loved, some replace lost loves with pets where they can find undivided love.

Scientists tell us a new love or a happy marriage relieves stress and can actually rewire the pain and past hurts. All through our lives the brain changes with new experiences. While being rejected hurts deeply and being in love makes one vulnerable, a good relationship can mend a broken heart.

Reach out to others with your caring and your love. I can't adequately express my love and appreciation to my faithful readers, as I attempt to share important aspects and experiences.

Stories cited: "A New Beginning" and "Music and the Senses" can be found in my publication "Musings", copyrighted 2012, by Amazon.com and Kindle. "Being Gaslighted" will be found in this book.

Cookies in the Oven

(The Mess Is Part of the Deal)

My Aunt Helen was a vivacious, auburn-haired secretary who loved life, loved dancing, and was such fun for me as I grew up. I only saw her once a year at vacation time, but I loved her carefree attitude and joy of life. Not until life became serious for me, as I brought up my four children and took on life's responsibilities, did I realize that Aunt Helen's style of living wasn't for me.

When my children were young and money was tight, I cooked and baked nourishing meals. During my twenty-five teaching years, there was little time for "fun-baking" with my school work and household chores. But, when I retired, I promised myself two pleasures. One was to relax and leisurely read the morning newspaper, and the second was to have fun with baking.

And so, holiday times, I took out recipes that had been collected and stashed in a scrapbook. I experimented and made cookies, cakes, pies, and had plenty of "mistakes along the way. But even that was fun because my family loved even the botched items. I made soups and stews and even tried "pot-pies" made from old recipes, and I loved the created results and even the messes to be cleaned up afterwards.

But, years later, Aunt Helen came up to Yonkers to visit me. I was shocked by her appearance. The cheery, optimistic girl I remembered was now weary-looking, showing insecurity and life's problems. Where had the joy gone? Life had worn her down. She had gotten married, but her two sons and husband were problems. The sparkle was gone from her face.

I write of this because, now that I'm old. I realize we all go through this at some time. The wealthiest, the most talented, all have those "down times". We look around and think others "have it made". But they don't. Behind those doors and handsome mansions there are always obstacles and "messes to clean up". To enjoy the cookies of life we usually have to work and clean up or "patch up" as we try and sometimes fail.

I Should Have Listened

(Paying the Price with Shingles)

How many times have I told children to listen? How many times have I warned friends to pay attention? How many times have I heeded good advice? But this time I didn't and I am sorry! Friends told me last year and again this past fall to get a Shingles Shot, that Shingles was an awful illness, to be avoided. And I kept putting off getting the shot. I didn't listen. And now I am sorry. I've had Shingles for over a week and don't see the end in sight for another week.

Over a week ago my right ear hurt, all around. I was afraid that I was getting a serious ear infection. That night I couldn't sleep with the pain around my ear, and the next morning I woke up with my ear and neck red, as though I had an allergy. Then I remembered eating too many of the delicious strawberries and thought of how foolish I was to overeat them, knowing I had "broken-out" in the past from over-indulging. Oh well, in a few days the rash would go, I thought.

But it didn't. That afternoon I went down to the skin allergist's office because the rash had spread and itched miserably. A soothing cream would be the answer, I thought. The doctor told me that I had contracted Shingles! It would be at least two weeks with this misery! I was put on prednisone and an anti-biotic and told to stay away from children and sick people and not to drive while on the prednisone! My world changed! I couldn't do the work I enjoyed, and I couldn't see my grandchildren, but, worst of all, my head pounded with deep throbbing headaches, all around the nerves of my scalp. I could barely rest my head on a soft pillow with the pain, and the itching and ugly sores developed, making me feel like a monster. Why had I been so stupid and not listened to warnings?

It has been a week of this horror. I have finished the meds and am now beginning to heal a little. My head still aches and I still can barely rest with a soft pillow, but at least I'm not on a perpetual "high" because of the prednisone's affect. I am haunted with the idea that I must write this "musing" to warn others to get that Shingles Shot.

According to my medical journals and my doctor, stress could have contributed to my body bringing on Shingles. Yes, I tend to overdo and get overtired. I don't like to stop a project until I feel it's finished correctly. But, above all, I never should have passed up the good advice given me. And I must write this to all of you who didn't get the shot.

As a child, I always felt having had Chicken Pox, I was now immune to getting it again. It was a real surprise to realize that in later years, this childhood disease could activate again. My medical bulletin says that anyone who has had Chicken Pox in the past can develop Shingles because it is caused by the same virus. The bulletin says that a temporary weakness in immunity may cause the virus to multiply and move along nerve fibers toward the skin and it is common in people over the age of 50. Illness, trauma, and stress may trigger this disease. It is less contagious than Chicken Pox. It is usually limited to an area on one side of the body and often comes with fever and/or headache. It usually clears on its own in a few weeks.

Getting the vaccine and the shot is what should be done to prevent all of this. Go to a local dermatologist and follow the advice you are given along with getting the shot. Don't be foolish and put it off like I did. Avoid the horrible weeks of suffering that I have had to go through. If only one reader listens to me it is well worth writing this column.

Inspiration

(Lincoln and Others)

What causes people to go into their "life path"? I often ask young children about their ambitions. Around ten or eleven they become sensitive to the world. I love hearing what they aspire to and why. Who or what entered their life to help that decision?

Recently reading the July 29, *New York Times,* I read an article that made me chuckle because it dovetailed with my theory of what guides children. It told of a writer, Harold Holzer, who has co-authored and edited forty-two books about Abraham Lincoln. Forty-two books! I can't imagine his being so deeply occupied with one man, even Lincoln. Most people admire Lincoln who grew up poor, with little formal education, reading books at night by candlelight and splitting logs during the day. He was a gangly homely man, with a sense of humor and a sense of justice that has inspired and fed the stories of numerous books, a man who changed our country. But Mr. Holzer, after forty-two books, still continues to write about Lincoln. Imagine being at a party with him. You wouldn't dare talk about Reagan or Jefferson or Clinton, anyone other than Lincoln. If I were his wife, I imagine everything around us would have to do with Lincoln, even trips, recreation, discussions. I do hope she also loves Lincoln.

But, what made me chuckle is the part that, as I sit here and type, it still has me grinning, is WHERE Mr. Holzer was inspired. Back in fifth grade, over fifty years ago, Holzer had to pick out a name from a hat to do a written report. He picked Lincoln and has been "on a kick" promoting, writing, theorizing, investigating him ever since! I wonder who his teacher was, and does she realize what she started in this man's life. There are "Lincoln junkies" and over 16,000 books written on Lincoln with no end in sight. There is a new movie out with Lincoln using his ax against vampires. I doubt though that anyone can top Holzer's record of books on Lincoln. (Holzer said his buddy in class picked Genghis Khan and "eventually became a rock'n'roll promoter". Is that what they call "luck of the draw"?)

But it is not so simple. Just as positive ambitions are formed in those crucial years, vengeful, cruel and mean ambitions can emerge. The parent who degrades the partner or the child, showing insensitivity, is teaching a life style. A parent's attitude can pave the way to confidence or to self-defeat. The relationship of parents is like a template or model for a child. The examples given at this young age can be the frame for his psyche. A person's self-image is often carried through a lifetime. Try overcoming a negative self-image. Sometimes a lifetime isn't long enough.

However, recently I asked a friend why he became an electrician. He said he hated school and had flunked most school subjects. When he was ten years old his father had an electric train set and he became fascinated at what powered the cars, how the power went from the rheostat to the trains. He used to lie on his belly and watch the trains starting and slowing down. His interest in those Lionel trains drove him to be a very successful electrician today.

130

I asked a young woman why she became a doctor, even though, when training, it was considered a man's profession. Her answer was the Dr. Kildare TV shows and the drama of a hospital with the excitement of treating and healing. Another young man, who I have written about in a former "musings", became intrigued at how words could influence and teach. He is now a prominent writer for a large New York paper.

You never know when you are an example. Your words, your smile, your interest in what they are saying could make the difference, especially to a child who is exploring ideas for his future. Your example shows children your concern or lack of concern for feelings. That fifth grade teacher, fifty years ago, started a man on a path to expertise in his knowledge of Lincoln. Maybe you will be the one to inspire someone to positive pursuits.

Life's Ironies

(Starting Over)

Why does it seem like the things, objects, feelings that we most value and desire are often taken away from us? There is the young girl who loves color, harmony, beauty, buys the house of her dreams and decorates it to perfection, only to have her only child destroy it with temper tantrums, making holes in walls, breaking antiques. There is the middle-aged woman who, with limited means, has treated herself, through many years, to lovely melodic CD's, to enrich her quiet moments, only to gradually lose her hearing, realizing she no longer can hear the pieces. And there is the artist, with growing macular degeneration, who is no longer able to properly mix her colors and convey the beauty that her mind visualizes.

What of the faded beauty, the woman with impeccable taste, the former envy of other women who had others copy her mannerisms and styles, who, reaching her fifties, develops cancer and loses her thick lovely hair? And what of the couple who found each other for the wrong reasons, she for his money, and he for someone to nurse him with his growing tumor? They live in a mansion, but only painfully endure the daily rituals of living together, despite being surrounded by luxury.

These are the ironies of life. We can have our goals, our dreams, and hours of hard work, all dashed down. All of our work for nothing! Ah, but that is the test! Can we rise above this? Can we "regroup", start over? Can we set new goals, maybe this time going about it in a different way, or do we sink in despair? Do we find our solace by going off into wrong, non-productive directions? There are all kinds of adages like, "Life is not a bowl of cherries!" and "The Best Things in Life Are Free!" I certainly don't know all the answers. All I know is, we can't let events and accidents and foolish mistakes deter us from going on, maybe in a different direction.

My hearing loss changed my life in many ways. My joy of singing for twenty years in the church choir was over. Even with excellent hearing aids, I couldn't hear the exact notes and tones of other singers, or even properly hear my own singing. In daily life, I missed out on the nuances and tones that people convey when they speak with special meanings. I found that I often misunderstood discussions, and I felt that I was being looked upon as growing senile.

But then, instead of talking, I started to write out my thoughts and feelings. I had become depressed with the hearing loss, but, by investing my thoughts in writing, I reached others with my ideas, and am now enjoying a totally different communication as well as new meanings of what I see and feel. Yes, even though many friends are surprised that I tell so much about myself, that I open up my past, I finally realize that sharing those past ups and downs has linked me with others who realize that they aren't alone. As some politician once said, "I feel your pain." And I really do.

Not just the hearing loss, but I have experienced so many disappointments and "start overs" that, when I say, "I know exactly how you feel", I really do. It really has been a tough journey, this living. But, no matter how bad it is, we must make ourselves start over each time, and we must especially help others who are starting over again, and give them a hug, and let them know you understand.

The Night Before the Holiday

(Too Tired to Sleep)

It's 3:00 AM and I can't sleep. I woke up about an hour ago. What's the sense of lying in bed thinking of preparations for the holiday? Since it's only "family" I don't have to impress anyone. But I am thinking of what I must still do, besides getting the turkey in the oven early enough.

All the vegetables are cut up and ready to cook. Giblets are in the refrigerator ready to cook up for gravy. I even baked the two pies, one especially gluten-free. But then, maybe little Nicole would like something chocolate to munch on while she sets up the crayons, paste, and assorted colored paper after the meal, keeping busy, as the rest of us continue talking over coffee. I think I'll make a fast brownie batch right after breakfast. There should be time before the turkey goes in.

The trouble with my mind is that, once I'm awake, my mind starts thinking. Sometimes it's over bills, sometimes someone I recently met, or even a recent article that intrigued me. Any of these can get me musing, and when I muse, it's often a story I'm compiling.

This "story thing" has become "compelling" to me. So many times, while talking to a friend, or even a new acquaintance, I think "Gee, that could be a great story." I never know what will claim the curiosity or interest of my readers. My stories go from past memories to anger and questioning the world and life today. The most "banal" subject causes readers to call or Email me. Who

135

would have thought my story about Peggy Lee would be prize-winning? Who would have thought writing about "Housedresses" would have stirred so many readers to call and tell me their experiences!

Here I am in my old cozy bathrobe and slippers. It's now 4:00 AM, and I'm drinking hot milk and eating cookies, and writing about my family coming, and I should be sleeping, or at least resting, before the excitement and joy of seeing them all, and knowing I'll be constantly on my feet until the turkey is done and all the vegetables are boiled, seasoned, and buttered. And then, much, much later, they'll help me clear the table and stack dishes for the dishwasher and probably have more coffee and cake before leaving. This is really the best part of their visit. I love those last comments and observations and even arguments. By the end of the meal everyone kind of "sits back" and pontificates, mellowed from the meal and feeling relaxed. This can only happen at home, I think. Being rushed out of a restaurant for the "next sittings" doesn't lend itself to these after-thoughts and casual observations that come when everyone knows where the others "stand" on local events and politics, and really honest and frank comments spill out. I know that I'll wish I had slept. But then, don't I always do this! Don't I always get my "motor revved up" too early in anticipation of the day!

Every year I say we should go out to eat. Then it would be easier for me. But I guess I must admit that it's still a challenge to me to make a mini-feast and later hear them all tell me how great my gravy was. And they tell me the pies were delicious, commenting that they are so much better when they are homemade.

Yes, I guess I am bragging! I can still put out a good meal at my old age. And we never know what another year will bring, do we?

Past As Prelude

(Family Narratives)

I am always interested in new psychological studies, especially concerning children. Two recent studies particularly captured my attention. The first one studied young children's vocabularies and their ability to communicate. The findings were that the more education the parents had, the more they talked to their children, and subsequently, the more the children talked. This could be for many reasons such as poorer parents being too busy to interact with their children during the day. They might not have family meals with discussions and sharing of the day's activities. This lack of communication limits children's vocabulary and limits children's discussions with their friends and development of vocabulary. Pre-kindergarten schooling is especially important for these children.

The second study, (*New York Times*, 3/17/13) "dove-tailed" with this first study, because it concluded that the more that the children knew their family histories, the more self-confident they were, and the more resilient they were to trauma and life's problems.

The psychologists call it "the family narrative" and it means the family's past and familial traditions. Children are better able to face life's challenges when they know where the grandparents came from, where the parents went to high school, family illnesses, even family tragedies. All kinds of stories and adventures should be shared such as where the parents met, and why past relatives came to America. Did they always live in this state? Did they always go to this church and were they always interested in politics?

The family narrative is called "ascending", when it discusses where the family came from, or "descending", for example, if the family used to be wealthy and then lost it. It also could be what they call "oscillating", the family's having had "ups and downs" and setbacks, but they stuck together and weathered it. Maybe they had lost everything in a flood and worked hard together to regain a new home, or maybe their family came over to this country penniless and are now important community members. Children can identify with the past and be proud of their heritage. All children love stories, and they especially love identifying with past relatives and their adventures.

A family that has core values helps their children to have pride and self-worth. They develop a strong identity and even a sense of their history. The psychologists stress that even "kooky" anecdotes help children relate to the family-past. This is especially important during adolescence when children are developing self-worth and belief in themselves. The parents' communication alone helps children to realize they are part of something bigger than themselves.

This study tested a large group of children who had all been through the same trauma, the 9/11 destruction in New York City. They found that those who knew their family histories were more able to cope with what they had recently gone through than the other children. A strong sense of family helps to give children a better sense of control over their own lives, resulting in emotional health and happiness.

In the past, families often felt ashamed of their poor grammar and knowledge of the English language. They sometimes would rather not tell of a past relative who had been arrested or who had embarrassed their family. But today we are taught to appreciate those who can speak other languages and we are finding that the past has rich stories to share. Knowing one's "family narrative" gives self-confidence and binds the family with the past and future generations. Every child should know the richness of their family-past, the troubles, successes, hopes and even dreams met, and their desirable goals for the future. Families should identify "family values" and instill them in their children. These studies have found this creates pride and builds up a child's self-worth and identity. They can know that their own adventures will add to the "family narrative".

Having Courage to Try New Things

(Being Vulnerable)

A dear friend, on reading a "Musings" article, said, "You are telling all kinds of things about yourself!" I wasn't sure if she was reproaching me or warning me to be careful, in letting past experiences and thoughts be opened to public criticism and scrutiny. On thinking about her comment, I realized that indeed she was a private person who people only knew on "face value" and she never showed emotion when expressing her ideas. She was pragmatic about everything, very sensible. Maybe she was right, I thought, but then, my pleasure in writing these musings is having readers tell me they have experienced many of the same adventures that I have. I like her ideas, but she doesn't show her feelings. And that's the pity! I admit that I love readers relating to my experiences.

Opening myself up to criticism is scary, but then, now that I am in my eighties, I see how unimportant criticism is, as long as I go into new avenues with good intentions. I was told that, after retiring from teaching, going into a new career of real estate was a mistake. I would be vulnerable to all kinds of bad experiences. I'd be going into strange houses, with people I'd never met, into neighborhoods that I would have to find, locations out of my county or district.

In many ways their warnings were right, but then, fortified with their thoughts, I was careful, working only locally, meeting with people who wanted to move into the county. My love of this beautiful countryside and my sincere welcoming of potential buyers only helped my work, and so, going against all warnings, I had a successful fifteen year career selling real estate. I met new friends, and I especially enjoyed selling new houses and condos. I loved helping buyers choose colors, carpets, and decorations. I created a quarterly newsletter for one of the local condo developments that was widely read and even sought out by other realtors. Even this was a new and successful venture for me, approaching potential buyers with my ideas and thoughts in a publication.

Another criticism from friends was my doing so much volunteer work, and getting no money for my efforts. But how can you measure the pleasure of seeing an aged, wrinkled face smile in delight because I played a ragtime upbeat song from her past, at a nursing home visit? How can you say I am not paid when a trembling hand grasps mine in gratitude for coming to visit, when she asks me to come back again soon? And when I see troubled, very sick patients cozily covered in lap robes that I have spent hours crocheting, I am happy and grateful that my fingers aren't arthritic with pain and that I am able to spend my TV hours making the crocheted creations. I've never been sorry that I freely give my time to volunteer work.

I was told by a well-meaning friend not to bother to publish my "Musings" collection of stories because it would only be a lot of work to publicize it, for gaining only a few dollars per book. She asked why I wanted to go further with a book when the "Musings" newspaper column was reaching so many, and the book would never become a best-seller! But no, I again let myself become vulnerable, venturing into printing the book and trying to publicize it myself. I once again risked disappointment in not knowing how it would turn out. But I was fortunate to be approached by a wonderful lady from Amazon Books who offered to help in the book's publication. Her encouragement and help resulted in my book "Musings", which now has been bought by countless happy readers who I meet everywhere I go! Yes, vulnerability takes courage, but it also can bring great rewards.

Today's Fashions

(What Goes Around Comes Around)

My sister and I used to love to play dress up with Mom's old clothes. I remember too, that back in the 1970's, kindergarten children "played house" with discarded clothes. But, I never thought that grown-up, fashion-conscious women would find "cast off clothing" to be "treasures". Now, even as in the past, our "stars" are the trendsetters who are discovering that they can set fashions and interpret style displays, and they are looking at the old "treasured outfits". Don't take my word for this. Go to Sunday Styles in *The New York Times*, (December 29, 2013).

I realize that the "torn-jeans look" has been popular, and the shirt hanging out from the jacket is also seen everywhere, even at Senior Citizen gatherings. It also is common for men these days to wear any kind of hat indoors, even throughout dinner. But I can't get over how the "sloppy" styles of today's youth are accepted and even adapted by older folk. When I read this article in *The Times* entitled "Trendsetter of 2013? Goodwill" by Guy Trebay, I was fascinated to read that worn out day-wear and "moth-bitten leopard-print mink" is what they call an "exuberant success" today. I felt compelled to keep reading on about our new "thrift-shop" culture. Apparently, even wealthy people are buying up old clothes from the Internet as well as spending hours picking out outfits at thrift shops to amaze and excite friends with their imaginations and fashion sense. And only recently, Designer Marc

Jacobs, retiring from Louis Vuitton, displayed an outfit of "dark lace and feathers worn with ratted-up jeans". At another show, faded, ripped jeans were seen with a $5,000 jacket from Chanel. And male models from Brunello Cucinelli wear "Duck Dynasty" beards.

Style-setters Rihanna and Miley Cyrus have been seen wearing such outfits as Balenciaga boots and gym shorts. Designers are saying that fashionable people are no longer restricted by any norm or trend. They prefer to interpret their own styles. "Onesies" and what are called "jail-bait shorts" worn with high-heeled Blahnik pumps were seen at the recent Marc Jacobs New York show. Flesh-displays are common, and the "dollar table" at the thrift shops hold golden possibilities for style-conscious young people today. Low neck blouses and low-riding shorts are common among those wanting to show off tattoos. Hip-hop, Rat Pack, Old Hollywood—are all good, possible styles says Michael Hainey, deputy editor of *GQ Magazine*.

A spokesman commenting on these styles says that our more "open culture" is causing this return to past fashions and attitudes of being controversial and different. Editors of fashion magazines say it is a more "open culture" today, meaning that there is more freedom in dressing.

In a former article of mine called "Hanging Out" (*The Putnam Times/Press*, 6/20/12) I concluded that by "letting it all hang out" there is less covering up of attitudes and feelings. We don't have to guess people's values anymore. We used to say that the clothes made the man. Now that it all "hangs out" we know immediately the kind of person we see and are involved with.

I don't know whether this trend is good or bad. I believe in individuality, but I still believe that something psychological happens, depending on what our outfit conveys. When we are dressed nicely, I think we tend to act nicely. Maybe in the old days clothes covered up who and what we really were. Maybe it's better that we know, up front, what a person really is, and whether we want them as friends or examples for our children.

Today's designers are inspired by the new openness in style, according to Mr. Hainey. Pajama bottoms worn as day-wear, old-fashioned discolored Grandma cardigans, old afghan blanket coats and see-through blouses, all make statements about our sense of worth, our belief in independence and thumbing our noses with tradition. It really is a "Brave New World".

Fifteen Hours as an Election Inspector

(I'd Do It Again)

It was Election Day, 2013, and up by 4:00 am, I packed my meals for a fifteen hour day at the polls. By 5:15 am, I was off. In the past, voting was in beautifully decorated rooms. This year's voting was in a 13x11 foot unfinished "shell", with ugly cement-block walls. The high, unfinished ceiling showed water and fuel pipes, mingled with wires. Rug squares covered more wires and the dusty cement floor. The room's only good features were the large windows across the front wall, giving us full vision of Main Street, and its "passing parade". Watching the comings and goings of local citizens would liven up the very long day.

We moved the voting booths closer to the windows so that the very tiny ballot words could be read. The overhead hanging bulbs were 12 feet above the tables and several were burnt out. Indeed, it was a depressing room, but the comments the voters and the staff blurted out turned it into a joke. "Very fine décor!" was heard. "This room looks like Rube Goldberg put it together," another said. "This is called 'Warehouse Style' décor", was heard. Most voters were appalled initially, but ended joking about it.

We asked headquarters for more lighting and the men soon came, installing portable light towers around the room. Light would be important to read the ballots. About 8:30 am, a car pulled up in front, smoke pouring from the hood, and a little old lady got out. Heavy fumes of acrid smoke billowed into the voting room.

147

Immediately, several of our inspectors rushed out to help, fearful of an explosion, and the policeman on duty called the fire department whose truck was there in minutes. We watched the wrecker arrive and "scoop up" the car. There had been a hole in the coolant hose. But, I don't remember the little lady coming in to vote.

Soon after, a "heavy set" man arrived, speaking only Spanish, waving a "Naturalization Certificate". He was intent on voting, but knew no English, and we couldn't verify his address. An interpreter was needed, and we called in a few Hispanic townsfolk to help, but no luck. Finally, the chairman contacted headquarters. They talked to the man, but with the language barrier, it took over a half hour to get his address and check whether he could vote with us. He wasn't registered, and he lived in Putnam Valley. We watched him jump into his car, which was parked in front, and drive off. Not knowing any English at all, what kind of license could he have to drive?

Around 10:30 am, a "Good Samaritan" left off three bags of candies for us. We appreciated this, because, by now we were thinking of food.

At 10:45 am, all the lights went out, caused by the "overloaded circuits" from the new portable lighting. "Emergency ballots" were brought out, but luckily not many voters came. The voting machine had to be "rebooted" they said, and this took over an hour.

From noon on, a steady flow of voters kept us busy, and we squeezed in eating our sandwiches and snacks. There was a wonderful distraction at 4:30 when a voter brought in her fourteen year old "mini-dog". He ran around, loving all the attention. By around 5:00 commuters arrived, and by 6:00 pm, after over eight hours, we were all getting restless. A constant flow of voters distracted our "growling stomachs". Each time a voter came in we were quiet, but, in between voters, we inspectors started sharing anecdotal stories, favorite pizza places, favorite recipes. We all had become friends after years of working together, and it was a relaxing and fun time, with this exhausting day.

There was only one real problem during the voting. At 7:30 pm one man insisted on "sharing ideas" with his wife as she voted. He refused to leave her, but finally, reluctantly, left her voting booth. He shook his head saying, "But I'm her husband!"

By 8:00 pm a woman came in to get her lost eyeglasses, and by 8:30 we started tallying materials for the election board and disassembling one of the election booths. All the signs, tags, poll books had to be accounted for. Some voter always comes in at exactly 9:00 pm, and so we couldn't pack everything. Promptly at 9:00 the entrance door was locked. It was detailed work, and none of us would leave until everything was tallied and in its proper "suitcase", ready for headquarters. What a tiring but productive day, but I'd do it again!

From Leggings to Stockings to Leggings

(Robin Hood Wore Them)

Yes, Robin Hood wore them, knights and king's guards wore them, and I wore them as a child. My mother had me wear my "leggings" in the winter. And now, even Catherine, the Duchess of Cambridge, wears them. This past fall of "2012" the new favorite accessory was to wear leggings. For the last few years, wearing pantyhose has been abandoned, and bare legs were favored, even for the most fashionable women. And now, leggings are "in".

Spanx has been a reliable body accessory, a real "tummy-tucker", and self-tanning lotions were perfect to conceal leg imperfections. With the very short dress styles in fashion, modesty now demands the current leggings that are in style. Even Lady Gaga, a current entertainer, has been wearing them. Often they aren't especially noticed because they look like sheer hose, and often they are made to slim and tone the legs. Some stars wear two pairs, one nude colored, and the second a "fishnet" stocking, for special effects. (I must insert, that, being now in my "senior years", I am not "into" these new styles of short, short skirts, low-bosomed tops, and leggings.)

I have read that leggings are not an inexpensive accessory. They are often sold for as much as $30 to $80 a pair, I have been told by reliable sources. They can come with stripes, with colored bands, with open-type weaves, and they are not uncomfortable to put on or to wear. They have even been known to help circulation.

Women with veins that show in their legs love the way their legs are covered with beautiful colors, patterns, and, best of all, they are in the latest style. Working moms and working women all love the compression that leggings offer those tiring long days on their feet. This wonderful new style suddenly offers beautiful shapely legs without having to do anything. No more going out on a winter evening, freezing, with bare legs. No more long preparation times for applying self-tanning lotions. Having an instant wardrobe of black leggings is handy, but colors and designs can set off an outfit, giving a new confidence and style to the wearer.

Whatever goes around comes around, someone once said. I didn't know what they were talking about. But now I know. I think of how cozy those old "Doctor Denton" pajamas were, with their feet attached, and these new leggings have even brought back that old cozy pajamas-fashion. I loved seeing them advertised recently, but they didn't give credit to Dr. Denton. (Of course, the new version didn't have the "flap-back" that my old ones had for going to the bathroom.)

As I look in the flyers from Neiman Marcus to Kmart, leggings are featured in all shades of colors, all prices for the rich as well as for everyone else.

Some have "bootcut fit", "leggings fit", even "capri fit", all to suit yoga, pilates, and training workouts. Most are "body-hugging for ideal performance", as the ads say. All offer excellent "mobility". Then there are styles in what are called "contemporary collections" named after movie stars. I found pink leggings, with black dots, and patterned and even footless leggings to be worn with flip-flops, as I perused the ads. Some were lilac or orange and others were opaque.

Ah, to be young again! A young friend recently said I should wear leggings! Yes, maybe under the slacks I have found to be comfortable, but I don't plan to wear today's stylish short dresses and blouses with low cut bodices. I certainly love the thought of the old Dr. Denton's at bedtime. I wouldn't have to wear socks to bed when it's cold!

But I will now have another look at the old Robin Hood movies.

Happy Endings

(Snack-Time Stories)

One of the nicest times of the day for my students as well as for me was "snack-time". Around 2:00 each day, when six hours of school had already gone by, we all looked forward to that 10-15 minute time when I read another chapter of the current book, and we all munched on our daily snack. I had favorite books that I read, and a particular one was Charlotte's Web, by E. B. White. I bring up that story today because recently I was talking to a friend about today's children's stories.

When we read a good story or book we are whisked away to another world, away from our current problems and conditions. A well-written story can be an inspiration and can even change our ambitions. Each year, for ten years, I read this book to first or second grade classes, depending on which grade I was teaching. And, without fail, when Charlotte died in the story, I couldn't hold back my own tears, because the story "touched me" so deeply. It spoke of friendships and dedication, and giving wholeheartedly to strongly held ideals. It was written in such a sweet, understanding way, with such logic and compassion that it always renewed my values of helping others. (The "watered-down" short version of this book doesn't have the power or the excellent writing of the original book.)

In today's world there are countless stories told to children in the media and at home, but how many teach perseverance, honesty, loyalty and faith? The better fairy tales, the ones my grandmother told me and I later read, impart core values. The familiar stories told in other cultures, the ones carried on from generation to generation, give messages of beliefs to the children, rules to live by.

Recently I reread The Happy Prince by Oscar Wilde. This story profoundly affected me when I first heard it read on a record. When I looked up the book on my computer, it was interesting to me that under the title of the book it said, "A story intended to be read to children". I was curious about this and again read the story, realizing that the author wanted "the reader" to get his message, not just the children who were being read to. (If you want to read this story, go to Google on your computer and bring it up.)

This memorable story tells of giving unselfishly to others, when, all the while, the sacrifice was not really being appreciated. It builds up the reader's sympathy for the giver, and, it has a powerful religious-type ending. This was written by the famous and infamous Oscar Wilde! As I read this story aloud to a friend recently, I literally choked up with emotion. Yes, even though I knew the ending, having read it many many years ago to my own children, it still overpowered me. The message is so beautifully written for the listening children, but it has even more poignancy for a thoughtful, concerned adult.

Why are we wasting our children's time with empty, foolish stories that are meaningless in terms of their needs, ambitions, values? They are better off lying on the grass, gazing at the clouds, or running around playing Tag or jumping rope. What happened to "Hop Scotch" and "Kick the Can" or making mud-pies? Even playing "Monopoly" or "Scrabble" is a better use of their time. Books and stories should be of value. They should be read and reread and kept in special bookcases. Or am I just old-fashioned? I love Kindle and Books-on-Line. But, even more, I love my old Grimm's and Anderson's Fairy Tales. Even Raggedy Ann and Andy books taught values. Have you looked at what children are immersed in today? What they are looking at on TV or what they are reading? Have you even looked at those violent "video-games"? Do you know what they are teaching our children? Have you thought about our culture's values?

"Rock Around the Clock"

(A Visit to Montrose Veterans' Hospital)

The small, pale man in the front wheel chair called out "Do you know my old favorite, 'You Are My Sunshine'?"

He was an invalid. The singing/line-dancing presentation had just finished and we were enjoying the cookies and lemonade the Montrose Hospital staff had provided for us. Pauline, our song leader called out, "Come on over here, girls, we have a special request." Still holding our cookies and paper cups, we clustered around him, and we joyfully sang out both verses of the old song, honoring the veteran's request. He knew he was being especially honored by us, and, with a big grin, told us how happy we had made him, hearing the old childhood song. It was a happy ending to a wonderful spring event, entertaining the veterans and their families at Montrose Veterans' Hospital.

We had entertained there before, but this visit topped all past performances. The entertainment hall was "chock full" of men and women veterans and the families that that visited them for the Easter/Passover holidays. Our group was bussed from the Mahopac Koehler Center Office for the Aging. We are all seniors, some even in their eighties, who regularly entertain at nursing homes and other senior centers. I have been the piano accompanist with this group for ten years, pulling out my old sheet music from way back, and programing and practicing the songs to be sung with the group. Rich Barnett tirelessly teaches line-dancing routines for the programs and practices with the dancers several mornings each week.

At the start of this performance, we passed out song-sheets, in case they wanted to join in with the singing, and it was really exciting, to hear the exuberance and pleasure in their voices. As each song finished there were rousing voices yelling out "terrific" and "right on" and "more, more"! The happiness that pervaded the very large entertainment room excited us all and made the singing all the more joyful.

In my "Musings" book I wrote that life can be like a two-scoop ice cream cone, the first scoop being the happiness we can give others by reaching out to help or give pleasure, and the second scoop being the joy we ourselves can experience in making life better. The Montrose program was so very special because this "full happiness" was genuine and deeply felt, that it was almost a tangible feeling for us all, performers and audience, alike. It's difficult to put into the right words, the warmth and camaraderie we all felt.

Not only was the singing exciting and appreciated, but the line-dancing was expertly performed, and the old songs like "Love Me or Leave Me", "Mack the Knife", and finally Bill Haley's "Rock Around the Clock" had the veterans bouncing around in their seats, their bodies keeping time with the dancers and their mouths forming the words to songs they recognized. Even the more exotic pieces like "Ann's Tango" had the audience moving along in time to the rhythms.

For more than twenty years I have been involved in various volunteer activities and I can't understand why every retired, and even those not yet retired, don't find their niche in some activity to reach out and help others who need a helping hand. I believe my crocheting afghans for donations or "lap-robes" for invalids can make life just a little better for someone. This dancing/singing group is a "two-scoop cone" for all, giving as well as receiving pleasure.

That small, pale invalid in the front row, made my day. All the way home on the bus and then in the car, I smiled to myself remembering "You Are My Sunshine" and even singing it, remembering his happy smile and the rousing voices of the audience joining our singing. I'd love to have the world "Rock Around the Clock" with the joy and togetherness that music can bring.

My Final Story

(It's Time to Try New Ventures)

After four years of writing "Musings" columns I'm planning new ventures and different writings. I never dreamed, back in 2010, that I'd be writing these stories or that they'd ever become my book "Musings". But now that I have another fifty-two, they are ready for the book, "More Musings With Dot". It's time for other writers to have the chance to be published here.

These four years of writing a column with the *Putnam Press/Times* have been fun and enlightening for me. I've been contacted by so many readers and have met scores of them. Strangers in the super market, when I'm shopping, have come over to give me a hug, after reading "The Magic of Touch". Former students have updated me on their careers and lives.

Two years ago, after reading my bi-weekly columns, an Amazon Publisher called me and offered to publish them in a book, "Musings". And now, with these last fifty-two stories, the book "More Musings With Dot" will again be published by Amazon. And this book should be ready by September.

Some of my favorites in the new book will be: "For Love of Country" (Lost Patriotism), "Remember Housedresses?" (Moms Wore Them), "It's Confirmed: Big Brother Is Watching" (Our "Brave New World"), "Poisoning Our Children" (Media Poison for Our Children), "Where Is Love?" (Relationships, with Benefits). As well as forty-seven more stories from my columns.

I will miss writing these stories. So often, as a discussion or event elicited memories, I'd say to myself (or even aloud), "That would make a great "Musings" story!" The more I wrote, the more old friends, remembrances, ideas, would come to mind.

Like the discussion about Fudgsicles lately, and how our little group all had great memories of them as kids. We remembered them as the perfect summer ice pop. Someone remembered they saw them recently on sale, and the rest of us were inspired to buy them at Shoprite the next day. And we did! See, even Fudgsicles gave us "conversation material" and something for me to write about. (I just took out time to have one now, caused by thinking about them.)

I was heartened by hearing that my sister-in-law, Betty, who lives in a local nursing home, uses stories from my "Musings" book for weekly discussions with her friends. Every Wednesday, I was told, she gathers a group of patients and they use one of my stories (or my essays) to start talking and comparing their thoughts. She says the nurses like them too and share the book with other patients. The stories are short enough, and yet all have something about feelings or past memories or the current culture to elicit a discussion.

One wonderful new friend, Linda, bought five books to give as "Stocking Stuffers" at Christmas. And, an ambulance driver I know asked if I was the author of "Musings" because one of his patients had a "Musings" book under her pillow when they arrived to take her to the hospital.

My "Book-Signings" were fun for me too. They gave me the input I needed for exploring new thoughts and different angles. To think someone in her eighties actually had something to offer that was thought-provoking, fascinated these groups. Hopefully, my stories have encouraged more seniors to engage in dialogs in expressing their feelings and ideas. Us old people are not all "addled" and maybe have good ideas from our long experiences that could encourage more discussions in families. Did their parents weather the Great Depression or World War II, or appreciate songstress Peggy Lee's musical talent? Did they eat at the New York Automat or have traveling salesmen deliver Fuller Brushes? Did they enjoy penny candy at the movies, or were they embarrassed by their first date the way I was? All these are in stories of mine. My stories are certainly eclectic!

They really are a "mixed bag" of subjects, and I have enjoyed writing them. It has been an adventure I am so grateful to have had. We never do know what the new day will hold, do we?

Acknowledgements:

-The local libraries for opening their conference rooms and providing refreshments for "book signings": The Brewster Public Library, The Kent Public Library, The North Salem Public Library and the Mahopac Public Library were all welcoming and supportive for these events.

-All my friends and the "Dancer/Singer RSVP Group" at the Koehler Senior Center in Mahopac, NY: They encouraged me, laughed with me, gave me new ideas, and made me feel like my stories "lightened their lives". (They also bought a lot of my books.)

-The St. Lawrence Seniors Group, The Putnam County Retired Teachers, and the Carmel/Mahopac Senior Drop-In Group who welcomed me at their meetings for reading my stories and book-signings.

-Vincent Dacquino who gave me the unique opportunity to talk about my stories to a TV audience, and boosted my ego by encouraging me to write a second book. He also invited me to be one of the "Meet the Authors" for the Public Library Writers Group.

- Eric Gross, Senior Editor and dear friend, who bought my first "Musings" book and wrote a wonderful article for *The Putnam Courier,* his newspaper, about my writings that went as far back as 2006 and 2007.

-And all my friends and relatives who bought "Musings" and encouraged and supported my new work with seniors.

-And SPECIAL thanks to my Publisher of *The Putnam Press/Times*, Donald Hall, and my Editor at *The Putnam Press/Times*, Holly Toll. There wouldn't be any "Musings" columns without their encouragement in giving me full literary freedom, and the printing of my bi-weekly "Musings" articles.

-And to my very dear friend and companion, Plinio J. Manoni who has encouraged me in all my endeavors.

About the Author
Dorothy H. Killackey

Dorothy H. Killackey was born in Pittsburgh, PA and earned a BA Degree in Psychology from Barnard College, Columbia University (Cum Laude). While raising her four children, she continued her education and was awarded an MS Degree in Education and later a 6th Year Professional Degree in Adult Education from Western Connecticut University (Cum Laude). She also was certified as a Child Developmental Examiner by Yale University.

As an elementary teacher, she taught in all the elementary grades for twenty-five years. Because of the education relevancy of her Masters' Degree Thesis on "Learning Disabilities", she was invited to conduct two teachers' workshops for the New York State Teachers in 1975 and 1976. She was the Teachers' Union President of her building and was on The Board of Directors at St. Lawrence O'Toole Parochial School (1974-76). She was a writer, lecturer, teacher to parents, teachers, and professional groups from 1972-82. In 1982 she published "Secrets of Learning", a newsletter for Grolier Publishers' Encyclopedias. In 1974 and 1989, she was awarded "Teacher of the Year", by the Brewster School District.

After retiring from teaching, while following a fifteen year second career in real estate, she wrote Old Timers' Biographies for the Putnam County Office for the Aging, was a member of the Putnam County Children's Committee, funded a writing contest for 7th and 8th graders at St. Lawrence O'Toole School, and established an "on-going" Killackey Scholarship for a graduating senior at Brewster High School. She was named "Senior Citizen of the Year 1999" by the Putnam County Office for the Aging, and in 2008 was honored with "A Certificate of Achievement" as the Putnam County senior giving the highest number of volunteer hours.

Dorothy served as president for four years for the local honorary international teachers' society, Delta Kappa Gamma International, and she wrote and edited their newsletter, "The Greek Gazette" from 1999-2007. In 2002 she became Coordinator of the newly formed SeniorNet Computer Program at the William Koehler Senior Center in Mahopac.

She has been on the RSVP Putnam County Senior Citizens Advisory Board since 2003 and has been piano accompanist since 2003 for the RSVP Dancer/Singers group that visits local nursing homes each week.

For the last two years, Dorothy has been writing her "Musings" column for *The Putnam Press/Times.* Her collection of stories/essays was published as a book, "Musings" and in Kindle by Amazon Publishers in 2012.

Made in the USA
Middletown, DE
19 October 2023

41101826R00096